She Just Wept

She Just Wept

Annette Rasp

To order additional copies of this book, contact:
Xlibris Corporation
1-888-795-4274
www.Xlibris.com
Orders@Xlibris.com
126007

CONTENTS

Dear Mia,

When you were two months old, I decided that I was going to start this letter of memoirs for you. Maybe I wrote these for my sanity and healing as much as I wrote them for you. I wrote them to give you insight into the past so that you could have healing in the future. You were born into such a world of turmoil, and if someday you need professional counseling, you can take these memoirs to the counselor to discuss. You had multiple strikes against you just being born. I'm sure that you have a greater risk of having issues since your mother was diagnosed with borderline personality disorder with severe bouts of depression and your father has ADHD.

Someday you will probably ask yourself, "Why do I have so much anxiety, and why do I struggle so much with my emotions?" And the answer really is in the past. I think that everyone gets caught between the past of things that happened and the future of whom God made us to be. Sometimes people get so caught on the negative of life that they can't see the bright future that lies ahead.

I know that not everyone will agree with my version of these memoirs or even my version of the stories. But these stories are my feelings and memories based on how I felt during these times of my life. I know that people think that it's best to keep secrets about how they feel, but I also know that the secrets of how we feel are what hold us back in life. I don't want that for you or your sister, Gracie. I want you and Gracie to remember your childhood for the good times, not the fighting. Over the years, I've learned that most fighting behavior is a learned behavior that gets passed down from generation to generation. Most times, we don't know how to stop it because we hold on to all the pain from the past. We hold on to insecurities from our earliest childhood years without realizing those are where the issues come from. We have pain that no one intended to put there, and sometimes the pain is so deep that no one realizes why they have no control over stopping it.

This book is my solution to help you to change your future. This book is not to point fingers of blame but to show you that we are all guilty of too many emotions, and sometimes we are guilty of loving too much. When we love people too much, we don't allow them to be who God created them to be because we want them to fit into a mold of who we think they should be. I pray every day for healing and change to happen in our family. I do believe that God is changing our future by healing the hurts of the past. I pray that this book does that for you, Gracie, and every other member of our family.

Love,

Nam

ANNETTE RASP

NAM

I WAS BORN into a small rural community where everyone knows everyone. Sometimes that is a good thing because it takes a community to raise a child. Other times it was a very hard thing because as soon as you made a mistake in life, everyone in the community knew it. To understand your mom means that you need to understand me and where I came from. I grew up as the middle child with two sisters, Hope and Sis. Life wasn't always easy for us not because we had it bad but because we lived the rural farm life, and we had no brothers. I'm sure it was harder on your great-grandfather to have three girls and no boys to run a farm, but our parents didn't miss a beat; they just taught us to work hard.

I look back at those days, and I realize how blessed we were growing up. We didn't have a lot of money, but we lived a relatively quiet life. My parents didn't discipline us by the usual ways. My fondest memories are of my dad yelling up the steps at us to go to sleep because 5:00 am comes early and picking rocks is hard work. Work was our form of discipline, but even picking rocks didn't stop my sisters and me from carrying on and talking half the night. There are very few times in my life that I can ever remember my parents fighting. There was never a time when I ever saw them raise a hand to each other. They taught us that we had to work together to keep the farm running. There was no "me and I" in our family because there wasn't time for that. Mom and Dad worked very hard to give us the items that they did give us, and we appreciated those things very much.

I was probably the biggest cause of hurt and pain in the family because I made a "mistake" at the age of fourteen, and this mistake probably caused more fighting within the family than any other thing up to this point in our lives. That mistake also became a source of great joy; that "mistake" was your aunt Sarah. You see, I became pregnant at fourteen and gave birth at fifteen, and thirty years ago, it was not as accepted as it is now. When I figured out I was pregnant, I hid it for almost four months, and I didn't tell anyone but the father. His response was to go out and rob the local diner so that I would go get an abortion, not exactly the response

I was hoping for. I sunk so low into depression that I tried to commit suicide by overdosing on some prescription pills. I figured that dying was better than being an embarrassment to my family. I didn't believe in abortion, so I decided that I would just end my life. I took the pills, and I sat on the floor all night crying and just waited to leave this earth, but that never happened. I know that I took enough pills, that something should have happened, but when morning came and nothing happened, I pulled myself together, and I had my first very real conversation with God. I had always attended church as a child, sometimes with my parents, but mostly with our neighbors, so I knew who God was in the intellectual sense. But this was the first time that I ever felt the true peace of God. I knew from that day forward that God had great plans for this child, your aunt Sarah. I walked down the steps, and I did the hardest thing I ever had to do. I told my parents.

In this day and age, there are lots of teen pregnancies, but back then, it turned everyone's world upside down. My parents had to fight to keep me in high school because I had two more years to go to graduate. The school wanted me to quit, and my parents were not going to allow that to happen. I did stay in school, and I did graduate. It wasn't easy being a single teen mother as well as going to school full-time. Plus I had to get a part-time job to help to pay for the babysitter, diapers, and other items that went with having a baby. My parents helped me, but they also reminded me that Sarah was my responsibility, not theirs. Aunt Sarah was quite the sickly baby. Right after she was born, she aspirated a bunch of mucus into her lungs. She almost died in the nursery that evening. If a visitor hadn't been walking past the nursery and noticed how blue she was turning, and started yelling for a nurse, she might not have made it. Back then, they put babies in the nurseries with glass windows for all to see. Now every newborn stays with the mother at all times.

Sarah developed a lot of lung and bronchitis problems for a couple of years. When she would have breathing issues or colic issues, I used to have to walk the floor a lot of nights. I believe the reason she loves to read is I had to read book after book to her as we walked the floor. The problem was, they weren't regular books. They were my schoolwork. I figured that she just liked to hear my voice, so I talked out loud and walked. By the time she would fall asleep, I would sit down and cry myself to sleep. Many nights I cried because of the pain I caused everyone, including myself, and other times I cried just because I was exhausted. Sometimes your aunts, Hope and Sis, would go into the room and take Sarah so that I could get caught up. I appreciated all their help because I might not have graduated if they hadn't helped me.

This is the time in my life when I truly struggled with who I was as a person as well as what I should do about the future. I wanted so bad to be a teacher because that had always been my dream, but no one encouraged it. Matter of fact, I had a school counselor tell me that my only goal now was to be a good parent, and she wouldn't even help me to fill out college applications. My parents just wanted me to get a job and take care of Sarah, so I gave up on my dream. I vowed to myself that I would educate her to the best of my ability. I vowed that I would try to encourage her to live life outside our small community and that I would teach her the birds and bees so that she would never be a teen mother herself. Sometimes I think I took this vow to myself too far as all three children will tell you. To the point of embarrassing them to death every time they had a boyfriend or girlfriend. I just never wanted them to live with the embarrassment and people's meanness that I had had to live with. Those pains were very hard to endure some days. I had to remind myself over and over that I deserved to be happy and to move forward in life.

I didn't date a lot after Sarah was born. There were only a few people that I even hung out with. People assume that because you have a child, you are a worthless person, and I was called many mean names like *tramp*, *slut*, and every other thing you can think of every time I did try to date someone besides Sarah's real father.

People seem to like to beat people who are already down. I think it makes them feel better about themselves. Years of negative comments take a toll on you, so you tend to stick to yourself. When Aunt Sarah was about a year and a half old, I started working at the local grocery store. This is where I met your grandfather, Jacob. He also worked there. For six months, he asked me out, and for six months, I said no. Not because he wasn't nice to me but because I didn't want the rumor mill to start again. His cousins also worked there, and they nagged and nagged me until I agreed to go on a date with him. We always had a really nice time, but when you are a teen mom, you always wonder in the back of your mind if the baby's father will come back. You always wonder if you are making the right decision to move on. This was an internal struggle that I had every time I dated. The longer I dated Jacob, the stronger that internal struggle was for me.

By now, Sarah's dad was living in Germany. Even though I knew in the back of my mind that he had gone there with his mother and stepfather to get out of the responsibility of paying child support, I decided to get on a plane and fly to Germany. I was seventeen years old, and your aunt Sarah was two years old at this time. This was really hard on my parents as well as my sisters. They couldn't understand why I would fly halfway around the world when Jacob wanted to marry me. I tried to explain to everyone that in your heart, there is always that belief that there is the perfect family especially when you grow up with parents that loved and respected each other. You just want to believe that the real father of the child is the best person to raise their child.

We went to Germany and stayed there for a month. In that month, I grew up a lot. I also realized that some people make choices not to grow up, that words are sometimes just words, and that all the promises of change were just words. My heart truly became broken for Sarah during that trip, but I knew that she would be better off being raised away from her real dad. I know that seems mean, but I didn't make that decision lightly. There was one big incident that made me realize how far apart we were in how we wanted Sarah raised. Here is the story:

Sarah was with her grandmother, and he had decided that we would attend this huge park event. There was food and tents for every country, and I was having such a good time, and he wanted me to meet his friends. We went to this area and started talking to some people, and the next thing I knew, this little group started smoking hash. Right there in the middle of this park with thousands of people, with police riding horses through the park, and all I can think of was that I was going to jail in Germany. I started thinking that I would never get back to the States and that I would never see Sarah or my family again. The more I think, the more I started to panic, and I lost it in front of all his friends. I started screaming at him to take me back to the house. I was screaming at him that I was going back to the States and never coming back. I was screaming at him that Sarah won't be raised this way. His response to my panic attack was to tell me to chill out and to get over it because if Sarah ever decides that she wants to do drugs, I need to understand that he will do them with her. He told me that I couldn't protect her forever. We were having this huge fight about drugs in the middle of a country with the strictest drug laws in the world. Eventually, he did take me back to the house, and I started packing my stuff and yelling at his mother that I wanted to go back to the States. Only to find out that they had only purchased a one-way ticket for me to get there. I went to the room and had another meltdown. This went on for the last two weeks of the trip because I just couldn't seem to get myself pulled together. Finally, his stepfather bought me a ticket back to the States. I

ANNETTE RASP

was sure that caused a war all in itself, but I didn't care; I just wanted to go home to people who loved me. This incident in the park opened me up to an understanding of drug addiction that I didn't have before. Through all the pain and hurt, I had come to understand that an addict will find drugs no matter where they go. Until they truly want a different lifestyle, no distance or change of location can change them. Change truly does only come from the inside out.

Even through all this, I still struggled with the thought of whether I hurt Sarah by keeping her from that family. In my heart, I have always felt that Sarah wouldn't be who she is today if she would have been forced to be split between two very different types of lifestyles and belief systems. I guess this is really a question that only God can answer. Sometimes I truly believe the scripture 2 Corinthians 6:14, which says, "Do not be unequally yoked together with unbelievers. For what fellowship has righteousness with lawlessness? And what communion has light with darkness?" Many preachers preach that this is about the color of our skin or the type of church that we attend. But I believe that lifestyles have a bigger impact on people's happiness. If one parent believes that it is OK to do drugs with their children, and the other is opposed to doing drugs altogether, how do you match those thought processes up? In my mind, you can't, so I walked away without looking back. I just wanted my daughter to be more than I ever was. More than her real dad was. He was the smartest person I had ever known, yet it all went down the toilet because of an addiction to drugs. I never wanted your aunt Sarah exposed to that or to the fighting that went on in that family. Mouth fighting is one thing, but I saw with my own eyes what physical abuse could do. Watching some of this physical fighting between Sarah's real grandmother and her real father's stepfather was appalling and left me shaken as a fifteen—to sixteen-year-old. I couldn't imagine what it would be like sending my daughter there every other weekend. All I know is that I tried my best to protect her, and it was never my intention to hurt her or his family.

As a side note, I carried a lot of guilt around on and off for years about terminating that family's rights, and in 2010, your cousin, Fred, had a four-wheeler accident, and I spent a lot of time at the Johnstown hospital with him and my sister, Hope. During that time, one of Sarah's real uncles spent the night at the hospital with us because his daughter had been dating Fred during this time. He came over to me at 2:00 am and asked if he could talk to me. I hadn't talked to any of them in probably twenty years, so I was a little surprised, but I agreed. He told me that he wanted me to know that he never blamed me for removing Sarah from their family. He told me that if he could have removed himself, he would have because the domestic violence, the drugs, and the anger had escalated over his teenage years. I told him about feeling guilty over the years.

He told me that he always thought of me as brave to fight to remove Sarah and that he always thought about Sarah and how lucky she was not to have to go there.

We talked for several hours about his life and Sarah's life. Sometimes it takes years to make peace with things from your past, but I truly did that night. You need to remember that you will never be perfect or make perfect decisions, but you do need to learn to forgive and move forward.

When I got back from Germany, Jacob and I started dating again. I knew that he loved me and Sarah, so we set a wedding date. Of course, my biggest fear was about the gossip that would occur when we told people that we were getting married. Because of my fears, Jacob and I decided that we would not have another child until we had been married at least a year. Plus, we started the adoption progress immediately after we were married. We wanted all our children to have the same name. Aunt Sarah had my name, and we wanted her to feel the same as would any other children that we would have.

It was a smart decision to wait on having more children because dating someone with a child is one thing, but moving in together with an instant family is another. It was a very hard transition, and the pressures of the families didn't help the situation any. No matter how much you think you know someone, living with them is totally different. I didn't realize how far apart Jacob's family and my family were. I assumed that because your grandfather's s parents had been married a long time, our families were alike. Don't ever assume anything. Where my parents didn't fight, Jacob's parents couldn't be in the same room as a family without raised voices and insults. I always felt like I was hated by them because of the fact that I already had a child, and once we were married, the insults started flowing my way. The problem was that I didn't know how to handle it, so I fought with Jacob a lot. I was always trying to force him to stand up for me. The problem was that he didn't know anything other than this loud, fighting attitude because you see, this was normal for him. It was very overwhelming to me, and I went into another stage of depression because I was convinced that everyone in Jacob's family hated me. I was so emotionally beaten up that I didn't realize how the negativity was affecting Sarah. Up to this point, Sarah only knew the calm, quiet farm life of my family. Sure, we had our fights as sisters, but we were also very close, and our dad and mom didn't tolerate too much fighting.

At three years old, Sarah went from being taken care of by everyone in the household to having a mother who was barely holding it together. From sleeping with me every night to being forced to grow up and sleep in a bed by herself. From having my undivided attention and me reading to her daily to me being overwhelmed with all that needed to be done to maintain a house by myself. It didn't help that Jacob's mother did everything for the men in the family, so I was expected to do the same. I felt that I went from a household of sharing responsibilities to a household of being responsible for everything and everyone. I felt like no matter where I turned, I was a failure at being both, a mother and a new wife.

ANNA

ANNA WAS CONCEIVED in the midst of all this turmoil and depression. I realize now how depressed I was, but back then I didn't really acknowledge it. I just thought it was normal to have so many mixed emotions about life. I just chalked it up to all the turmoil that always seemed to be going on since we lived in the house beside your great-grandparents' on your grandfather Jacob's side.

Anna has always been a handful for us, and I've always felt bad to a degree that most of her insecurity came from me. When she was born, I went through a pretty bad bout of depression, and I really struggled with her. Besides being depressed, Anna, unlike you, was a very needy baby. She always wanted to be held plus we tried many types of baby formulas, and none of them agreed with her. I look back at it now and realize that she was stressed as a baby. Being stressed even as a baby can cause lots of stomach problems; to this day, she gets an upset stomach when she is stressed out.

Jacob, on the other hand, was good with Anna as a baby. I don't think he understood the depression, but he understood that I needed help. At this point in our life, I was only working part-time, and he was working construction. Every morning, he would feed and diaper Anna before he went to work at 4:00 am so that she would sleep and I could sleep. It meant so much to me that he did that every day even when he didn't have to go to work. Even with the extra sleep, I was so overwhelmed with her daily care and keeping track of Sarah, who was getting ready to start school for the first time.

By the time Jacob got off work, I was shoving Anna out the door at him. He was working ten to twelve hours a day every day, but he would take Anna and sit on the swing with her for hours after work. Most times, I just went to sleep on the couch. What he also didn't know was that I had already napped when she did earlier in the day. By the time Anna was six weeks old, I was more than ready to go back to work part-time. It actually was the best thing because I worked in the hospital nursing home as a CNA, and one day, when my family doctor was doing patient rounds, he pulled me aside and started talking to me. He had noticed my depression right away and sent me to get some tests done. When the blood tests came back, he told me I had hypothyroidism as well as he felt that I needed an antidepressant. I was twenty years old. This was the very first time I admitted my depression issues, and I did start a medicine for it.

The other issue we were fighting about at that time was babysitting. Jacob wanted his mother to babysit, and I didn't want her to. Not because I didn't like her or think she wouldn't do a good job with the girls but because they were already having a say about every decision that went on in our marriage. Jacob didn't make a decision about anything without asking them their opinion first. I felt like his parents hated me with all the negative comments they made about me; add that to the depression, and they were my enemies. In the end, I gave in because we really didn't have the money to pay a babysitter, and she was willing to babysit for free. In some ways, I regret allowing your great-grandmother to babysit all the time because of the lack of respect they had for me. My feelings weren't important to them, and they probably, to this day, have no true understanding of how their negative comments affected my whole family. It was a learned behavior that they passed down from generation to generation without even realizing the effects. They were not physical fighters, just verbal, but sometimes verbal is worse than being smacked. But I also know now that some of my feelings were out of proportion with the truth, but when you don't like yourself, it's hard to see things the way they really are.

Over the course of Anna's life, there was always the stress of whom to listen to. Since your great-grandmother babysat her when she was little, she developed this attitude of "I don't have to listen to you." Any time she didn't want to do what I said, she would take off and run down to Grandma and tell them I was being mean to her. Then Gram would call up and scold me for fighting with her. This was quite a cycle of contention between Jacob and me. I know that your mom and Sarah never truly understood why we fought, but it was a matter of what I felt was respect. One piece of advice for you: don't live beside your parents or in-laws when you get married unless you are positive that your husband will stand behind you first. If your husband-to-be doesn't understand that up front, then don't marry him because he isn't ready to be truly committed to his new family. Even the Bible tells us in Ephesians 5:31 "that a man shall leave his father and his mother and be joined to his wife and the two shall become one flesh"; that is a little hard to do when one of the people holds their parent's opinions higher than those of the person they married. It has taken Pappy and me years to get our independence from their advice and influence since we still live beside them twenty-seven years later. Time and age definitely help all situations.

I was twenty when Anna was born, and there was so much turmoil going on that I started back to church every other weekend when I wasn't working. I felt that church was the answer to immediate change of the problems and issues. That doesn't happen because it takes years for change to happen in someone, and it only comes if you really want change. I became quite the religious fanatic for a while. I quit drinking and decided that I wanted no parts of the partying group. This caused as much trouble, between Jacob and me, as the drinking did. First, we fought because we both drank, then we fought because Jacob thought I was too good to hang out with old friends. What he didn't understand was the changes I was going through and that I was barely hanging on emotionally. I just wanted peace. Peace with my family, who didn't drink and growled me for it. Peace with his family, who blamed me for everything. Peace with myself for feeling like a failure as a mother. Peace with myself for failure at being a good wife. Sitting in church was the only place I felt any peace during these years of my life. I truly felt that if I didn't stop drinking and fighting, I would need to get a divorce, and I wasn't ready to give up on my marriage.

Over the years, I have truly learned that there is a difference between religion and relationship when it comes to God. I have learned that my relationship is my walk alone. No two people will ever have the same walk because God created us each differently. The Bible tells us that God knew us before we were born.

To me that means he knew me and loved me for me way before all the mess of life took place. I know that I didn't always walk in the path that he probably wanted me to go, but I know that he has always been there to guide me through the mess I created. Sometimes God allows us to go through the mess because he knows that is the only way we will change and want something different. As parents and grandparents, we have a tendency to want to protect from the fall of errors when sometimes the fall is what truly changes people. I know that I have had many experiences over my life to know without a doubt that God is real, but I also learned that you can't push those experiences on others. You can tell your story and your experiences, but only that person can decide if they believe in God or not.

Even with all the conflict, Anna's true emotional problems didn't start until after her accident. Sometimes we can look back on things and realize where the real issues start. It's too bad we can't see them at that time. Don't get me wrong; your mother, Anna, was always a little bullheaded. One time when she was three years old, it took me over one hour to get to Hagerstown because I had to stop the car five times to put her back into her car seat. No amount of growling or spanking would keep her in that seat. She also used to crawl under the tables and fuss when we went out to eat. It was so bad that your grandfather and I quit going out to eat because I don't know who acted worse—your grandfather, who got mad at her, or Anna, who wouldn't come out from under the tables—so I gave up on the going out. We started ordering take-out food and staying home.

I was at work the day your mother had an accident. She was about eight years old, and she had been playing with her male cousins in the yard. They had been jumping on and off the picnic table when she fell and did a split right over the edge of the table. The trauma was great. When she hit the corner of picnic table, it caused her to give herself an episiotomy. That is a very private injury, and she started bleeding profusely and then she passed out. The boys had to carry her to Jacob. Of course, your grandfather had to look to figure out where the bleeding was coming from, and he had to take her to the hospital. At the hospital, she received a male doctor and then a male surgeon. I believe that all this poking and probing by all these men before she even got to see Mom was probably very emotionally overwhelming. Several months after this accident, your mom started having other behavioral issues. Anna couldn't seem to be happy with anything. We had conflict after conflict over clothes, hair, and anything else that she didn't think was perfect. There were mornings that I would be late for work because I could put her hair in a ponytail twenty times, and it still was not perfect. Her clothes also had to match to the T. If the shade of color was off even by one tiny bit, she would refuse to wear them. It got to the point that we had to remove all her clothes from the bedroom except for two outfits. The fewer choices she had, the better.

I believe that having this accident made her feel imperfect, so she couldn't seem to make peace with herself about anything. I didn't see all that back then. Back then I was just overwhelmed with her bad attitude. Poor Aunt Sarah was always on the receiving end of your mom's bad behavior. Aunt Sarah used to call me, crying all the time in the morning because she couldn't get your mom ready for school. Your mom didn't cooperate with Sarah much. I was always so torn by what to do. I couldn't financially afford to leave work every time Sarah called me, yet I knew it wasn't fair for Sarah to have to deal with your mom's Dr. Jekyll/Mr. Hyde mentality. I switched jobs, hoping that my going to work later would help with the morning routine. Not realizing that the afternoon routine would become the same mess as the morning one was. I was always so torn by what to do with Anna that I made an appointment to take her to a counselor. That option did not go over well with either your mom or Jacob. I stuck to my guns, but I ended up in tears every session. At nine and ten years of age, your mom knew how to tear me apart before we ever got to the counselor. Anna always had the ability to have me in tears on the way to the counselor, but I'll never forget the time that we walked into the doctor's office, and I had been crying, and the counselor asked us if everything was OK. Anna said, "You better take her first, she is the one that is nuts, look at her crying." Honestly, over the years, Anna has made me feel like I am nuts. She really makes me wonder sometimes if I really am crazy. On the other hand, I probably got more out of counseling than she ever did.

Anna's counselor, Dr. James, told me one time that children are influenced 25 percent by their genetics and 75 percent by their surroundings. He told me that Anna had learned her disrespect because of the family surroundings in which she was raised. He also told me that if I divorced your grandfather, Anna would never forgive me. Divorce was a serious consideration for me at that time, but I prayed a lot, and I listened to this counselor and did what he told me to do, which was to find my voice. Back then, I was very soft-spoken, a lot like your aunt Sis. Dr. James told me, the only way for me to help Anna was for me to change. He said that I had to learn to take a stand. I needed to hold both Anna and your grandfather Jacob accountable for their treatment of me. He also told me to stop taking their behavior personally and realize that it is learned behavior. It has taken me years to realize what a learned behavior is. Learned behavior is very hard to unlearn because most people don't realize how they come off because it is their normal behavior.

Anna and I went to behavioral counselors three different sets of times over the course of her teenage years. Each time, I think I learned more and changed more than she did. I also did individual counseling with a pastor and a different counselor. I was also on anti-depression medicines through several of these years. Just remember that counseling can be a good thing if you get people you can trust. It can give you the insight that families aren't able to have because they are too close to the situation. I was also influenced by a couple of very strong women at this time in my life. God really does send helpers. Most times we don't realize that until years after the fact.

Hopefully, Anna will remember some of the words of counseling as she gets older, but back then, she still chose to get into drugs and alcohol. Anna

ANNETTE RASP

could have been a huge leader of something positive in school, but she chose to be a follower. We fought over grades, friends, curfews, and everything else that she didn't like about me. I'm sure that Sarah was very happy to be in college by now, and your mom never tried to have a relationship with her brother, Ryan. Uncle Ryan's goal in life was always to stay out of her way. It saddens me that to this day, they don't have a relationship, but I know how Ryan feels because during her rebellious stage of drugs, alcohol, and fighting, sometimes I wished I could have disowned her too. It's hard to love and forgive over and over again when all the words spoken are hateful.

Here are a couple of incidents from her childhood that really stick in my memory. The first one was during her softball-playing years. When Sarah was old enough to play softball, I was talked into coaching one of the teams. I started out coaching Sarah, but the year that Anna was old enough to play, she started out playing for a different coach, and that did not go well. Anna thought she knew more than the coach, and the coach couldn't handle her. By the end of the first season, we had to move Anna up to my team. So the next year, I gave up coaching Sarah so that I could coach Anna. Believe me when I say we butted heads a lot. Your mother's birthday always fell in the middle of the season, so one year, I think she was turning ten, I planned a surprise birthday party for her. After the game, I allowed the team and their parents to get to the ice-cream shop before we did. Everything was set up with balloons, cake, and ice cream, and when it was time for Anna to walk into the room, everyone yelled "Surprise!" She took one look around and looked at me and said, "I am not having my birthday with these people," turned around and walked out of the restaurant and locked herself into the car. I looked at the people and said, "Let's eat." We ate cake and ice cream, and your mother never did go into the party. How many ten-year-olds wouldn't be happy for a party? I learned my lesson, and from that day on, I never planned any surprises for Anna. I learned that Anna always needs time to process upcoming events.

Another big incident that sticks in my mind was when she was fifteen or just turned sixteen. By this time, she was already running with bad kids and doing drugs. I didn't know that then. I just knew that she thought she didn't have to listen to me, and she thought that if she pushed me enough, she could get her way. But the mouth on her was horrible, and when she was younger, the counselor taught me a counting process to use with Anna. It was basically a way to tell her that she was crossing the line. If I counted one, it was a warning. Then I would count two and tell her what was going to happen next. Then I would mostly send her to her bedroom, or sometimes I would have to go lock myself in mine. Then I would count three and give her a true punishment, like take something from her, ground her, or sometimes paddle her butt. It worked well when she was younger, but on this particular day, her mouth was more than I could take, so when I said two, I told her that I was going to smack her in the mouth if she said one more nasty word to me. She didn't believe me and got into my face, calling me every name in the book, so I backhanded her in the mouth as hard as I could. Needless to say, she shut up and went to her room, more out of shock than anything. But she couldn't let it go that I had hit her, so the next day after school, one of her friends took her to the county children's service to report me. The guy from children's services drove her home and came to the door. He wanted to have a conversation with me about what had happened. I looked him in the eyes and told him that he could have her. "Just give me the papers, and I'll sign them, but before you take her, I just want you to do one thing. I want you to stand up, and Anna will talk to you like she talked to me." He stood up, and Anna said some of what she said, and I said, "No, Anna. Put all the anger and curse words into it," so she did. That's the thing about your mother; if she is confronted or told to do something point-blank, she will. I think it has something to do with being very black-and-white when she thinks she is right and you are wrong. She will do what you ask, not realizing how bad she sounds. When she got done talking, the guy looked at me and said, "I would have done more than busted her in the mouth. This case is closed, and I won't be coming back for any follow-ups. I hope things get better with you two." Then he walked out the door, and I never saw him again. I asked your mother if she thought they would take her. I also told her, if she ever did that again, I would gladly sign her over to them. It didn't stop her mouth from running, but things did calm down for a little while.

The next big event I remember was the fight. Who would have thought that I would have to referee a fight in a parking lot in Deer Run. Anna and this girl had been mouth-fighting for months, and on this particular day, they decided that they were going to meet and have it out. I always told Anna to call me if she was ever angry enough to fight. My thought was that I could talk her out of it. That didn't work so well. I pulled into the parking lot, and there must have been twenty-five cars and fifty teens there. My first thought was to yell at everyone to go home, but I walked over to Anna, and she was ready to fight. I looked over at the girl, and she had her mother and whole family standing there, egging them on. I asked them both if they were seriously going to fight, and I reminded this girl that she was two years older than Anna, which made her an adult because Anna was sixteen. I also told her that I know my daughter, and if I let Anna fight her, she would get beaten up, and it won't be a fair fight because Anna has anger issues. This girl's family kept insisting to let them fight, so I said OK, but no one was allowed to break it up but me. I gave my word to fifty people that we would not press legal charges, and everyone gave their word that no one would interfere. I told the girl that she had to swing first because that would ensure that she didn't file charges whenever Anna beat the crap out of her, which I assured her was what would happen. She swung at Anna and missed. The next thing I knew, Anna was beating the crap out of her. This girl was six feet tall, and Anna was only five feet, but Anna already had her on the ground, beating her head off the blacktop. The family was screaming at me to make Anna stop. I looked at them and said, "Are you sure this is the end, and you all will stay away from my daughter?" They were screaming, "Yes, yes. Just get her off her before she kills her." I walked over and pulled Anna off her. Just then the state police went rolling in the parking lot, and all the teens started hopping in their cars and running away. I would not allow Anna or the other girl's family to leave until I talked to the state police. I told them the truth and that it would never happen again. They left us all, leaving with only a warning.

Anna's senior year was even more coated with drugs, and with the drugs came more fighting and more emotional meltdowns. Every day I regretted our decision not to medicate her at a young age for her mental health issues. Every day was a fight of some sort. By the time graduation was upon us, we had all had enough. There was a huge blowup between us all two weeks before your mother, Anna was to graduate, and we ended up giving your mother a choice: to get clean or to get out. We had had a big fight over her continually breaking the curfew rule. Anna had decided that she didn't have to listen to us, and she wouldn't come home on time. One night, your grandfather, Jacob tried to take her cell phone as punishment. Anna was not giving up her phone, and it turned into a physical fight between them. I thought for sure your grandfather was going to put her through the wall that day because when he tried to take her phone, she went at him with both fists swinging. She called him every name in the book. It took all he had to subdue her. This was probably the first time that I seriously thought about calling the police on her and having her carted off. Your grandfather never did get the phone from her, but he told her that she was grounded and had to be home immediately after school or work until after graduation. Later that evening, she came down the steps and announced that she was leaving, and she would be back later. She took off out the door so fast that neither of us could stop her. When she didn't come home, we got very concerned. We had tried to call her repeatedly, but she either hung up or mouthed off. She called your grandfather and me every name in the book that night and informed us that she wasn't coming home, and we couldn't make her. I called her and told her that if she didn't come home within an hour, I was packing her stuff, and she could leave and never come back. I told her that I had had enough. Your grandfather decided to call the state police to ask them for help. They asked for her phone number and said that they would try to call her. I'll never forget what that officer told us that night. He did get a hold of her, and she told him to "go fuck yourself" and that he would never find her, so he could just mind his own business. When he called us back, he told us how she had talked and acted, and he said that he only had one piece of advice for us: follow through with throwing her out. He said that teenagers who get into drugs and alcohol this badly only change when you follow through with cutting them off. He said that it would be the hardest thing that we ever did, but he felt that she had no respect for us or authority, so let her fail. Those are very hard words to swallow at three in the morning, but Ryan had been up all night with us, worrying. Your grandfather and I talked to Ryan about what we were going to do with following the officer's advice. We also discussed how she was an adult, and maybe it was time to let her lie in the bed she had created. As a parent, you never want your children to fail, but you also can't let the wild child set the example for the younger one either. Both your grandfather and I cried most of the night, but we decided together that Anna would get help or leave. The next day, Anna came home as if nothing had happened. We told her that her clothes were packed and to be gone by the time we got back from our motorcycle ride. I have always felt bad because Sarah had come home, and we told her what was going on, and after we left on the bike, Sarah and Anna got into a huge fight. Sarah is the one who actually took her clothes and put them in the car and told her to leave. Apparently, Anna didn't believe that we meant it, and Sarah forced the issue. It really wasn't Sarah's place to have to do that, but I think she knew that none of us could take any more. I have always respected and loved Sarah for standing up for us when we couldn't do it anymore. She was in college at that time and didn't have to get involved, but she did, and it gave me the courage to stand firm with the decision. Those weeks leading up to graduation were the hardest. Every day the school counselor called me on Anna's behalf, and every day I told her *no*, that Anna could not come home unless she got clean, that I had to stand firm for Ryan's sake. Every day I cried at work because I felt like the worst parent in the world. Every day I beat myself up over being a bad parent, but every day I stood firm because of Sarah and Ryan. I knew that if Sarah thought it was the right thing, then I needed to stand firm.

There were many days when I was barely functioning on the inside, but I never left on to others what was going on within my household.

In some ways, I realized that we must have taught Anna something right because she did drive over forty miles one way to school every day from Waynesboro to Deer Run for two weeks so that she could graduate. She did this even while she was doing cocaine, drinking, and who knows what else. She also kept her job at the local food joint. I realized how much she was struggling with who she was and who she wanted to become, but I also knew that I couldn't help her with that struggle.

Graduation came and went, but things didn't get any better between her and me. I honestly didn't want her to move back home because it was quiet with her gone. I had so much anger at this stage of our relationship that it was easier to pretend that she didn't exist than it was to admit the truth. I could just pretend that she was healthy when I didn't have to look at her every day. Anna was gone for about six months. She didn't start RN school in August like she was supposed to. Most of the time she was gone, I didn't even bother to ask what she was doing with her life. When I did talk to her, I would just tell her that she had a home to come to when she was ready to get clean; otherwise, she couldn't come back. She told everybody how I threw her out. When people called, asking me about Anna, I always told them the truth: that she had a choice, and she chose a boy and doing drugs over her family.

Late one night, she came knocking on the door. She had bruises on her hands and arms as well as some blood on her. I opened the door and asked her what she was doing. She told me that she wanted to come home and get clean. She proceeded to tell me how her boyfriend, Max, had cheated on her and they fought when he broke her phone. She told me that she was pretty sure that she had broken his nose and given him two black eyes. I took her in that night, knowing that it was going to be a hard road back to being clean. It didn't happen overnight. She didn't go back to Waynesboro, but she picked up with others locally who were doing drugs. She was in and out of our house for about two months. During that time, she did make plans to go to LPN school and was accepted into the community college program.

In January, I had knee surgery, and Anna would come to the house and sleep on the couch for hours. Most days, I just watched her sleep, and I would sit there and pray for her. At this point in our lives, I really didn't think that anything I said mattered, so I just left her alone unless she asked me something. Anna was so depressed and thin at that time. I really worried about how she would start LPN school in a month. She just couldn't seem to help herself out of this mess that she had herself in. One day, I hobbled over to the couch and asked her if I could pray with her. I think that was the day that God helped us both, me to forgive her and her to realize that she was loved. I truly believe that God touched her that day in a special way because she did pull herself off that couch and she did start school on time. I was so proud of her because I knew it took everything within her to accomplish getting that LPN degree and to stay clean for that year. Anna learned a lot about herself that year of school. I watched her grow up in many ways as well as acknowledge that she had some mental health issues that only she could control.

Once your mom, Anna got her LPN degree, she started working as a nurse at the County prison. Having that job apparently helped her to meet up with some old friends, your dad, as well as some others from her high school graduation year. This started another round of drinking, which included an underage DUI, which cost her around $500. She also lost her license for three months. For three months, I drove her back and forth to work before I went to work myself. For three months, I lectured her daily the whole way over and the whole way back. I told her that this was the one and only time I would do this for her. I told her not to call me if she got in any more legal trouble, because we would let her sit in jail.

She also started bringing people to the house again in the middle of the night, and the 2:00 am fights started all over again. One night, she caused $800 worth of damage to a new car of some boy she was fighting with. After she damaged his car, she was trying to throw him off our property. He, of course, wanted to call the police, and a huge fight broke out among all the people outside. Anna came flying into our bedroom at 2:00 am to tell us to get these people off her property. When Jacob went outside to break it up, Anna got furious with us for telling the boy that she would pay for the vehicle. Your grandfather told him to get us an estimate for the damage, and we would get him the money from Anna to fix it. Anna got so mad that she went after your grandfather with both fists swinging, and he slammed her into the tree, trying to get her off him. I have no idea what she was on that night, but I know this: she is one mean drunk, druggie, or whatever you call her. I can say that night, I was truly scared that your grandfather was going to seriously hurt her. All these late-night incidents were taking both a physical and emotional toll on us. But no matter what Anna did, we tried to reinforce that everything she damaged, she would pay for repairs even if we had to have her arrested on our own property.

MIA

I MET YOUR dad for the first time in November of 2007. Anna came barreling into our bedroom at 2:00 am, demanding that I get up and go find David. Apparently, David had nowhere to stay because the person who gave him his home plan and helped to get him out of jail, had thrown him out that day. He and Anna had become friends, and she had been allowing him to stay at our house without our knowledge. They had been drinking, and I have no idea where they got the alcohol because they were both minors. They had gotten into a huge fight, which resulted in a pushing match between them. He had walked off down Route 16, and she was afraid that if he was picked up by the police, he would go back to jail for violating probation for using both drugs and alcohol. I found him at the local convenience store in Deer Run. I took both him and Anna to my house and told them to sleep it off and no more fighting, or I would call the police myself.

Later we found out that Anna had been dragging him to our house for weeks even though she knew that boys staying overnight with her was not permitted. She would sneak David (and sometimes others) into our house late at night and take him somewhere later in the day while we were at work. We had been through multiple issues with Anna in the past with bringing people home, but since she had been clean, we didn't think to check her room anymore. We always had this cycle of trust and betrayal going on. Just when we would start to trust her again and think that she understood the house rules, she would break them.

The weekend before Christmas 2007, Anna and David were again drinking and fighting. This night, David took Anna's cell phone and smashed it on the ground. Anna and David were in a screaming match in our driveway. Anna went barreling into our bedroom again at 2:00 am to tell us that David walked off with her car keys and that we needed to go get them back. While Jacob was driving around looking for David, I was trying to calm Anna down. She was intoxicated and mad. The next thing I knew, she walked out to the kitchen and punched a hole in the wall. Jacob found David and took him back to our house. David was also intoxicated. Jacob called David's dad and told him to go get him. While we were waiting, we asked them both what was all over the driveway. Apparently, besides breaking Anna's cell phone, David threw a pumpkin pie at Anna. He missed her, but he smashed some other personal items of Anna's that had been in her car. She, in return, smashed some of his items and threw them all over Route 16 for the traffic to run over.

After this incident, we informed Anna, David, and his dad, Ralph, that we would call the police with the next incident. We told them that we weren't going to go sleepless every weekend because of them. The next day, Anna took some of her clothes and moved in with David and Ralph. I was really upset about this because Anna had worked so hard for the past year to finally straighten herself up, and I could just see her life and her self-esteem going down the toilet. Some days I really wish she would have never met up with your father again, but then I remind myself that I wouldn't have you and Gracie. I love you both very, very much, and I would never give you back. I seriously think that Anna thought she could help your dad, but they brought each other down instead. She went right back into the drinking and drugs. I know that it was her choice, but I also know that Anna is not a very strong person emotionally. She uses fighting and anger to cover up her insecurities, but deep down she is hurting too.

One day in the very early morning hours, I woke up from a dream, sobbing and crying. I believe with all my heart that God gave me this dream as a warning to Anna. I saw her standing at a crossroads. On one side of the road, she would have peace and happiness, and on the other side, Anna stood holding a baby girl (which happened to be you). Not only was there a baby, but there was also pain and lots of it. As I was sitting in the bathroom, crying, Anna walked in. For some reason, she had come home that night to sleep. She asked me what I was crying about, and I told her the dream, and I begged her to change her life. I begged her to walk away from David and move back home. She cried with me and told me not to worry. But many times, I imagine her telling David the dream and laughing at me because that is how Anna is. She is quick to tell you what you want to hear, but she can also be quick to be cruel. Sometimes I don't think she means to be, but other times I wonder. Aunt Sarah always said she was like living with Dr. Jekyll and Mr. Hyde. Someday you will have to sit down with Aunt Sarah and ask her what it was like growing up with Anna. There are times when she has so much love and affection that you have to push her off you, and then there are times when she could kill you just for looking at her wrong.

Sometimes I wonder why God gave me this dream if he knew that Anna was going to choose this path anyway. The funny thing is that this dream wasn't the first mention of things to come. About a month before this dream, both your grandfather Jacob and I went to church to hear a special speaker, Pastor Allen, who gave us a prophetic word. He told us that we would have a child in our future. A child who would be a miracle yet would be surrounded with heartache. I assumed that he was talking about our current situation with Anna and a miracle of healing from drugs. Your grandfather, on the other hand, said that this preacher must be crazy or confused because we weren't having any more children. It wasn't physically possible since I had had a hysterectomy at twenty-seven. Both of us just kind of laughed it off until I had the dream. Then it sunk in to me that God was showing us what was coming. Your grandfather, on the other hand, wasn't much of a believer in dreams and prophetic words.

About two months after my dream, your grandfather and I received a call from Ralph at 3:00 am. Why Anna always had to fight in the middle of the night is beyond me, but she definitely caused us many sleepless nights. Anyway, he wanted us to go to Williamson to pick up Anna. Apparently, both of your parents were drinking and doing who knows what else, and your father punched Anna in the face. Then feeling guilty, he called the police on himself. They picked him up and took him off to jail. Anna, being drunk and depressed, walked into the kitchen and slit her wrist with a butcher knife. She will say that she did it out of anger, but she also cuts herself inside her thighs and on her lower stomach areas when she is depressed or stressed out. The doctors say that it is a way for some people to "relieve" stress. Not sure how that would relieve stress. It would cause stress for me. Anyway, she was sitting on the floor, bleeding, when your grandfather Ralph called us. I told him to call an ambulance because I wasn't hunting for his trailer in the middle of the night. When we got to the hospital, Anna was sitting on the bed, laughing, and said, "I didn't mean to cut myself so deep. I was just mad at David." The doctors were going to let her go home, but I told them that she had a history of cutting and drug abuse and that I wasn't taking her home. I told them that she needed help that we couldn't give her. The doctor checked her out and found fresh cuts on her thighs as well as the wrist, so he told her that she had two options. One was to commit herself for a seventy-two-hour hold at a rehab/mental health facility, or they would go to the courts in the morning to get me power of attorney so that I could commit her. She looked at that doctor to see if he was serious, then she said, "I'll commit myself because if she is in charge, I'll never get back out." She knew that I would make her stay there a very long, long time. Anna ended up being in the facility for ten days, and in there was where she found out that she was pregnant with you. Heck of a way to bring a baby into the world—drunk and fighting. I have a feeling that was how you were conceived, so please don't make the same mistake. Please take the time to meet a wonderful man who has wonderful values and only have a child when you are emotionally and physically healthy.

By the way, your dad was in jail for only seven days, which is way less than he should have gotten especially since he was already on probation for multiple assault charges. Someday you will have to get the details about all that from your dad or grandfather Ralph. Hopefully, he will tell you the truth and not sugarcoat it.

When I found out that Anna was pregnant with you, I begged her to walk away from David and to never tell him that she was pregnant. I knew in my heart that this was the true start to the long road of pain and misery, not because she was pregnant but because I knew she would go back to David. I truly didn't feel that your dad was ready to be a father, and Anna was surely not in control of her life. I also have a huge issue with men hitting women. I was raised to believe that there is absolutely no excuse in it. I know that women hit men and that is wrong also, but men physically have a lot more strength. Plus he hit her in the face; that, to me, is a true sign of anger. Of course, I was right, and she went right back to David. Apparently, none of the counseling while she was in treatment meant anything, but then the sessions that we went to when she was younger never meant much to her either. There is a lot of truth in the saying that you can lead a horse to water, but you can't make it drink. People who aren't ready to change don't listen. You can't change anyone but yourself, so don't bother forcing that issue. You can guide others and you can try to sway them to your way of thinking, but they have a choice just as you have a choice. We are each responsible for our own selves, so try to always make good decisions. Your mother reacts to most things in anger before she thinks, but I struggle every time there is physical fighting going on in her life. I have struggled many times over whether I should hire a lawyer and take you girls from her. Your parents did beat on each other. They said the meanest things to each other, and then just like that, they would pretend that it didn't happen. But while they are pretending that it didn't really happen, they are really building up to the next big blowup. Each blowup gets bigger than the next because you can only pretend so much that those mean words don't hurt. Each time they pretended that nothing happened, I wondered if I was the crazy one. I thought maybe I really did make up the past twenty-four hours straight where I was taking phone calls from your mom. Maybe I made up being cussed at and crying for all the pain that I had felt coming off Anna. I pray every day that you don't ever have to get sucked into that. It hurts so much to be pulled through this time and time again. How do you choose between trying to save your daughter or trying to protect your grandchildren?

I decided that my way to protect you would be to document everything just in case I needed to fight in court to get custody of you. I decided that I would include all those notes into this memoir exactly as I typed them up over the course of your first year of life. Mostly because I want you to read how it was for me and the family then, not how I might alter them now four years later. I honestly see some things differently now because I know and understand more, but back then I wrote based on my feelings and what I heard. Some of these have already been mentioned, but I had typed these up and printed them as I went along, so I had no copies but what I had printed.

*　　*　　*

6-01-2008: Anna woke her dad and me up at 2:30 am to ask us to drive her to the state police barracks in Deer Run. Anna told us that she had picked David up after she got off work, and he had been at a party and was intoxicated. They got into a big fight as she was driving him back to his dad's house in Williamson. She said that as their fighting increased, she told him to shut up, or she was going to drive him to the state police since he was violating his parole. This caused him to go crazy. For some reason, he had been sitting in the backseat of the car, and he started kicking the inside of the door as hard as he could as Anna was driving down the road at sixty miles an hour. He kicked the passenger door so hard that it flew open and damaged the door. When Anna stopped the car to shut the door, she said that David shoved her to the ground and kicked her. She was four months pregnant at that time. Anna had visible cuts and bruises on her arms and legs from being pushed on the blacktop. We drove her to the state police barracks, and she wrote up a report, but she refused to press the charges for assault. The state police in our County faxed the report to the neighboring County, but nothing was ever done to David. He promised to pay for the car, but he never did, so in December of 2008, I filed a claim with our insurance company so that we could get the car fixed. There was $2,099.89 worth of damage.

*   *   *

6-08: Anna and David continued to live with Ralph in Williamson. I received multiple calls almost daily about their fighting. I continued to encourage Anna to leave, but she wouldn't. When Anna was seven months pregnant, she told me a story about David smacking her in the head and shoving her into the closet. When he shoved her in the closet, she said that her head bounced off the wall. Anna calls me all the time and tells me how bad David treats her, but she will never leave. I wish I knew why. All I can think is that it is her own depression that holds her there.

*   *   *

11-08: The week before you were to be born, your dad quit his job. Who knows why. The thing I have realized about David is that he didn't need a reason to get mad, and he was forever quitting things. It's like he doesn't know how or he doesn't want to improve his life. I think that he thinks it's easier to let others do everything for him. The problem with that is that you will never learn to like yourself that way. You never get self-esteem by using others. Good hard work is always the best way to feel good about yourself especially when you do it for others. Anyway, your dad quitting his job and your mom being off work because she had you put more stress on their relationship than either of them could handle. The sad part is that all of us thought we were helping by stopping by and dropping off food. Your aunt Sarah even came to visit, planning to stay with them for a couple of weeks. But none of that was appreciated by your parents, and Sarah was so hurt emotionally that I ended up driving back home much earlier than she wanted to go back. Sarah cried almost the whole way back. She said that she needed me to drive her back that night, that she needed to go home to her husband, who loved and appreciated her. She was so heartbroken to see how your dad and mother interacted with each other. My heart broke for her because she wasn't used to this mess we called life. I feel that your dad saw Sarah as a threat instead of a help. Anna was so overwhelmed by your father's anger over us all being around that she chose to push us away also. It was hard for all of us because we wanted to help with you so much, yet we felt like we were never wanted. I realize that our family isn't like most and that we tend to move in and take over whenever we have a new baby or sick family member. But we do it because we love you all so much, not because we wanted to hurt or put anyone down.

After that night, the whole family stepped back from Anna and David to give him the space that he said he needed. He blamed our family and especially me for interfering in his role as father. He said that he couldn't bond with you because we were always there. But the truth of the matter was that I didn't go out unless Anna called me especially after I had to drive Sarah home. I stayed away even some nights when Anna did call just because I was mad at your father for the way he was treating my family.

*   *   *

11-12-2008: Mia is one week old. Anna called me, crying hysterically. They were fighting. She kept saying that she didn't know what set him off this time. I could hear him in the background, screaming at her. He was saying, "Having a baby with you is the biggest fucking mistake of my life. Take that baby with you, and get the hell out of here." I told Anna that I would be out in fifteen minutes because that was how long it took to get there. Anna just kept saying "No, just stay on the phone and he'll start calming down." As I was talking to Anna, I could hear him in the background, knocking things over. After about a half hour, he calmed down. The whole time all this was going on, poor little Mia was crying in the background. Anna was crying on the phone as well. She wouldn't leave, and she was afraid if I showed up, something worse would happen. The next day, I asked Anna what was he throwing around, and she told me that he had been kicking the baby furniture around and that he had broken Mia's baby swing.

*   *   *

11-18-2008: Mia is two weeks old. Anna called us at 2:30 am. David was on another rampage. I could hear him in the background, screaming at her to take the baby and get the hell out. David had called his mother, and she was there also. She was in the background, telling Anna to tell us to take a truck and get all her stuff out. Anna and Mia were both sobbing and crying. We left immediately. When we arrived at around 3:00 am, both Joan and David were gone. Anna and Mia were both on the couch, crying.

ANNETTE RASP

Anna had fingerprints around her neck, and she told us that he tried to choke her and then he slammed her against the wall. We had a hard time getting Mia to calm down that night. We packed up as much as we could, and we moved them home. Anna and I went back out the next day and moved the rest of their belongings.

*   *   *

11-21-2008: David finally called and asked to see Mia. He came to our house. I sat them both down and told them that I wouldn't tolerate any more violence in their lives especially since they have Mia to think about. I asked David why he would take a hold of Anna, and he admitted that he did. He said that Anna pushed him verbally until he lost it. Since that day, it has been like an emotional roller coaster between Anna and David. They fight, they break cell phones. They push each other around, and then they get back together again. They have been staying at multiple locations with Mia. I keep trying to tell Anna that they need to give Mia stability. Anna is depressed, and she is pushing Mia away. Anna sleeps on the couch when they are fighting, and I tend to Mia. I've asked them both to just give me custody for Mia's sake. This goes on for months.

*   *   *

I cried every time I had to go get you and your mom. I made up my mind that I would do whatever I had to do to protect you. For over three weeks, I cared for you every evening while Anna fought through her depression. Some nights she helped care for you. Most nights she handed you to me as soon as I stepped in the door from work. That was very hard for me because it reminded me of my own depression when she was a baby. It is a very lonely thing to go through, and I know that she wanted for David to change and to want you and her. Over the course of the couple of months that you lived with us on and off, Anna and David fought constantly. Some days I was so furious with Anna because I always felt that she thought David was more important than you. Other nights I sat and watched her sleep on the couch, and I felt so sorry for her because all she wanted was a perfect family. But you can't have perfect families with imperfect people.

Somewhere in all this fighting, Anna decided to get pregnant again. Once again, I knew before she told me. I'll never forget the day she called to tell me. She said, "I have something to tell you," and I said, "You're pregnant, and it is going to be another girl." And this time, because I was furious with God and her, I told her that God would never give her or him a boy because they couldn't appreciate the beautiful baby they already had. I was furious because why was God allowing this to happen? I realize now that the truth is, we were all born with free will, and sometimes God allows us to make our own mistakes. I cried for months over this baby girl. For many nights, I sat in the bathtub at night and cried because I was afraid this baby wouldn't be born healthy. I knew that Anna didn't eat right on top of the fact that she would randomly do drugs when she was mad at David. I don't think she fully comprehended that she was hurting the baby more than she was hurting David. Emotionally, I was struggling just about as much as Anna was. I had to go back to the doctor to get back on an antidepressant myself. I felt that if I couldn't hold it together, how could I help her?

I have always felt that Anna getting pregnant was intentional because David wanted a boy (like girls weren't good enough), and I felt that Anna thought, if she had a boy, she would have the perfect family and all their issues would go away. She thought that having a son would make David happy and he would change. The problem is that you don't always get what you want, and as soon as they found out that it was, in fact, another girl, the fighting started all over again. This time, your dad smashed and broke another baby swing. This time I called children's service and your dad's probation officer on the both of them. By now, I was worrying all the time about your safety. I decided that since they weren't listening to me, maybe, just maybe, they would listen to the law. This time, your grandmother Joan also asked them to move out of her house. You were four months old when Anna and you moved out. Your grandmother Joan has never seen you since. She has also never seen your beautiful little sister, Gracie. I don't understand how people make decisions like that. I guess sometimes it is easier to pretend that you don't have children that have caused you pain. Don't ever be mad at her for not being there for you girls. You have always had more than enough family and love to make up for her choosing to not see you.

During some of this time, we did get a break from the fighting. Your dad went to church with me for about six weeks. I honestly believe that was the only six weeks that they didn't fight violently. I had no desire to ask him to help with my church event, but Anna reminded me that I teach forgiveness all the time, so I need to practice what I preached. I know without a doubt that God can change people, but first, people have to admit that they want to be changed. I invited him and David fit right into my youth group, and one day, David went up to the front of the church for prayer. When we prayed with him, I believed with all my heart that he wanted to be different. My heart was broken more for him than he would ever realize. I wanted so much for them both to change for your sake. Yet they both went back to fighting within six weeks. I was so mad at them both. I have come to realize that nothing is in our timing, but God's, and I pray that they both will get complete peace from their demons someday.

Anna and David moved to an apartment in Deer Run, and things continued to escalate. Some days were quiet, and some days I cried all the time as I drove back and forth from place to place to pick up either you or Anna or both. The fighting was almost daily, based on the neighbors. Sometimes one of them would call us and tell us that Anna and David had fought all night and that they could hear Anna crying all night long. A couple of times, I went to the bank beside the first apartment and was told that Anna and David had been caught on the video camera pushing each other around. Most times you, Mia, were in your mother's arms while this was going on. We even got a phone call from the apartment owner, asking us if we knew that Anna was in an abusive relationship. He also told us that he was going to talk to them, and if it didn't stop, he was going to have to evict them. I had people approach me at work, telling me that they saw my daughter with a baby in her arms, fighting with her boyfriend on the street late at night. Your pappy and I went to the police several times to ask them what we should do. Each and every time they told us to call children's services and David's probation officer. They said that they couldn't do anything unless the neighbors called in a complaint while they were fighting. The police told us to go talk to the neighbors and ask them to call and file a complaint. We started doing everything they told us to do.

Yet not one person would file a complaint. Two of the neighbors were too afraid of how your dad might retaliate. Others felt it was not their place to get involved. Some people would ask me, "Why doesn't your daughter leave him?" and I would respond the same way I always did with "I don't know." I would ask them, "How can you watch and hear domestic violence and not care enough to call the police?" After a while, those neighbors stopped calling me because I was starting to be the angry one—angry at them for not caring enough to intervene. How does domestic violence ever stop if no one is brave enough to stand up to it by calling for help?

I felt that I had no choice but to contact your dad's probation officer and to call children's services on both of your parents again. It is the hardest and the saddest thing I have ever had to do, but I knew that every time I went to the apartment, things got worse, so I decided that I would have to take another approach. I hoped that this approach would help everyone involved. I knew that children's services had the legal right to drug-test your mother and possibly your father. I knew that they would encourage parenting classes as well as wellness classes. I also hoped that the counselor would be someone who could possibly talk to Anna and help her through the abuse. Believe me when I say it was not an easy decision nor was it easy being screamed at by Anna after they left. But in the end, it did help to calm down their fighting. Plus it was the only way that I knew to take myself out of the middle of their fighting. I couldn't go there anymore. It was taking such an emotional toll on me that I had to find a way to get off the merry-go-round that we were on. I prayed every day that your dad would be so worried about going back to jail that he would also calm down.

Here are several of the several letters that I wrote, begging for help. As well as some of my notes from this time in our lives:

To Mia's caseworker,

I am writing this just as an FYI because I know that you are still following the family situation of my granddaughter, Mia, and I want you to know some of the current things that are going on so that you don't drop them as a case. I have real concern for my granddaughter, and I want you to know that if something does arise, I will take Mia immediately any time of the day or night.

Here are some things that are going on in this family situation.

First, they just moved to Deer Run this past week. Their new address is 117 South Second Street, Apartment B, Deer Run, Philadelphia 17233. This is the building right beside the Democrat office and the Tower Bank.

Second, the fighting between Anna and David has been escalating to the point where David has hit Anna and then ran off a couple of times, but of course, Anna goes after him and drags him back. A couple of weeks ago, David hit Anna, and she came home to stay at our house for several days, and in those several days, I found out two things. First, David is not taking the medicine that his doctor prescribed him for his mental illness because he doesn't believe that he has a problem; Anna is the problem (so he says). Anna told me that David is considered a severe bipolar with severe ADHD and that he needs to be on medications to control his fits of anger. She also told me that the reason he hit her was because he was stealing money from her because he was buying and using heroin. If you go to his probation officer, you will find out this is true. I called him when all this happened, and David tested "hot." Yet County Probation refused to send him to jail. They told the probation officer to get him into rehab. I have no idea why this young man is allowed to violate his probation over and over again and nothing ever happens.

Third, my other major concern is that Anna is also doing drugs even though she is pregnant. Based on the phone calls to me and her behavior, her father and I confronted her about this issue, and she made the comment that marijuana helps with her morning sickness and that it won't hurt her. Needless to say, her dad and I went through the roof, and we informed her that we will not tolerate her putting our grandchildren into danger. We have people keeping an eye on both David and Anna, and we know for a fact that David purchased drugs as recently as Easter weekend. Anna was not raised this way, and I know that she has her own mental illness issues to deal with, but this is not the way to deal with them.

I know that you have the authority to test Anna, and I wish you would even if it's through one of her doctor's appointments with her midwife for this pregnancy. Even if she doesn't test "hot," at least she will know that she is being watched. Nothing her dad and I say seems to have an impact on her. I know that she has to go to counseling, and I pray that she turns her life around, but in the meantime, I worry about my granddaughter's safety. I worry constantly that the police will pick both Anna and David up one of these times for either the fighting or the drugs, and I want everyone to know that I will take Mia and raise her. If I thought I had a good case, I would hire a lawyer today to take her away from them both. Mia is such a sweet baby, and what will all this fighting and stress do to her? I know what it is doing to me, and I don't live with them every day.

The only time I don't worry is on the weekends when Anna works, and I watch Mia. I normally have her every weekend from Friday night to Monday morning, but I have to be very careful of what I say, or David tries to convince Anna that I shouldn't babysit That's why they can't know that it's me giving you more information because Anna has already threatened me with never seeing Mia again. But I don't know what else to do because babies can't live like this, and what about the baby she is carrying? What if she really is doing drugs, and it's not just her covering for David and his drug purchases? I'm just at such a loss that I don't know what to do. I want to thank you for keeping them in the system, and I pray that you continue to follow up even when they tell you things are good. There have been no good times for the sixteen months that they have been together. If you ever need to contact me, please feel free to call me anytime.

Sincerely,

Sam

*   *   *

5-8-2009: My sister Hope called me at work. She asked me if I could leave work and go to David and Anna's apartment. Apparently, children's services showed up for a surprise visit, and when they left, David went crazy on Anna. When she called Hope, Anna wanted Jake (her cousin) to go to the apartment. Hope asked her if David was hitting her, and she said, "What isn't he doing to me?" She called me immediately, and I left work sometime around two o'clock. When I got down there, David was screaming at Anna and packing his personal items because he was leaving. Mia was in her jumpy seat, crying, and both of them were ignoring her. I called Anna's cell phone and told her to open the door. I walked over and picked up Mia to calm her down. I told them both to shut up and grow up.

I gave them quite a lecture about why children's services would be there, including the fact that the place was a mess and there have been lots of druggie friends going in and out of that apartment all the time. Plus I told David that if I knew that he was in Anna's car behind the apartment, smoking dope, I'm sure that other people, including his neighbors, did also. I also confronted him about buying drugs in the dollar-store parking lot over the Easter weekend, and he didn't deny any of it. He said that he knew that he had a problem, and so did probation, so why didn't I back off and quit calling them? I asked him if they knew that he was also doing heroin, and he said yes. That was why he had to go back to drug and alcohol classes in Williamson. Then he turned toward Anna, and he said, "Tell your mom

     ANNETTE RASP

about your doing crack to get even with me for doing heroin." I looked at Anna, and she didn't deny it; she just kept crying. She would have been four months pregnant at the time. He also accused her of smoking weed, which she also didn't deny. I looked at them both, and I said, "And you wonder why I would call children's services on you two? Neither one of you are fit to raise babies." I then asked David to leave for a while so that I could help Anna clean the apartment. We worked at it for about six hours, and it was still messy. While David was gone, Anna admitted that he had been pushing her around and pulling her hair. All this fighting was going on while Mia was in the room.

The next day, David went back, and they both acted like nothing happened. This is how it is. They fight, they beat on each other, and they do drugs together all in front of my granddaughter. What do I do?

LETTER TO DAVID'S PROBATION OFFICER

11-2009

Dear Samantha,

I am sending you this information because I want you to know the David that I know. I know that there probably isn't much you can do to help me or my family because I have come to the conclusion that no matter what people do to other people, the laws really don't protect the innocent. Every time I think I have my daughter convinced to file a PFA or harassment charge against David, we found out that she could end up being fined or countercharged with something, so she always refuses to follow through because David has already cost her so much this past year, both moneywise and in terms of mental stability. I honestly believe that this is the reason that David can always get her to try again in their very unstable relationship. I keep praying that Anna will actually stick with therapy this time, and she will see the emotional damage that this young man is doing to all of us, not just her. It is very hard to watch your daughter be abused mentally and physically and just keep your mouth shut because you are afraid that opening it will put her in more danger, but all that changed when Mia was born two and a half months ago. You want to allow your adult children to be adults and to live their lives however they want, but since the birth of Mia, I have come to realize that some adults don't deserve to have children especially if they can't put the needs of their children first. My granddaughter doesn't deserve to be put into the middle of their fighting. She deserves more in life, and I need to protect her even if it means taking her away from both David and Anna. I sat through a counseling session with Anna at Women in Need, and I was shocked to learn of the violence that David has used against her. I knew of the incidents that I documented, but I was amazed at how much Anna really did keep from us. I was also shocked to learn from Women in Need that statistically, it takes at least seven times for an abused woman to leave her abuser. My question is, what if my granddaughter doesn't make it through that many times? What if the next time they are fighting, David actually uses his illegal handgun to shoot Anna? What if he actually breaks Anna's neck the next time he slams her against the wall? What if he loses his temper with Mia like he does with his dog, and he beats her and throws her down the steps like he did Caliber? Every day, I have so many what-ifs running through my head that it's hard to concentrate.

And every time I called a lawyer to discuss options about getting custody of Mia, they would tell me that, basically, Mia has no rights. They tell me to start documenting everything and to start informing probation every time there is an incident. They tell me to contact children's services every time Anna goes back to him even if it is only for a few days just so people know what is going on and can do home visits. They tell me to call the police, but what good is that if Anna won't follow through or even if they do show up, and David only gets a slap on the wrist for his violations? Here are just a few incidents that I know the police were involved in:

1. He was intoxicated, and he punched my daughter in the face, called the police on himself, and only did ten days in jail. My daughter did ten days in Roxbury.
2. He did $2,099 worth of damage to Anna's car while he was drunk, and he shoved Anna to the ground and kicked her when she was four months pregnant, and the night it happened, Franklin County wouldn't even go pick him up, so the next day, David talked Anna into dropping the charges. After the charges were dropped, he refused to pay to fix the car, so the insurance company is now filing a suit against him for the damages, and he just laughs because he says that since Anna dropped the charges, there is nothing they can do to get their money. He is wrong; the car and the car insurance are both in my name as primary owner.
3. He got pulled over for driving without a license at Christmastime, and all he got was a $400 fine, which his father paid for him. Driving Anna's car has been an issue since day one; my husband has had multiple conversations with both David and Anna about this. Anna lets him drive because she says that it isn't worth the fight.

Anyway, I am sending you all my notes so that you can read just some of the things that my husband and I have gone through since the day we met David. These notes don't even begin to tell the whole story. Both my husband and I have heard him threatening our daughter over the phone many times. You see, she uses me as a way to calm David down. Every time he starts with her, she will call me and tell me she is coming home. Normally, one of two things happens when she calls: either he will calm down, and he will let her leave, or he will break her cell phone so that she can't call me back, and I have to drive to wherever they are to make sure that my daughter is OK. Of course, he always leaves before we get there.

Since Anna and Mia have moved in with us, he realizes that he is losing some of his control over Anna. She has filed for custody with limited visitation, and she filed for child support, so now he has been threatening to take Mia from us. He has been telling Anna that he will not go back to jail, that he will run first. He says that he has nothing to lose, so he might as well skip the state, and he'll take Mia with him. I hope that he is only telling her this, hoping that she will drop the custody and child support, but to be truthful, I think he will run because his dad happens to work with my husband, and he has made several comments about he'll do whatever it takes to keep David out of jail even if it means taking David out of the state. Considering his dad is an alcoholic and is the person who supplies David with his alcohol and really doesn't have any ties to the area, but David, I think he might just do it.

Anyway, I will be more than willing to discuss any of this information with you. I know that this is a lot of information, and I know that David will deny everything especially about having illegal handguns, but I know he has them because he showed them to my sixteen-year-old son one time when Anna and David were living together. Plus Anna told me how he obtained them.

Thank you for reading and documenting my complaints about David.

*   *   *

When David and Anna moved to the second apartment, I was sure that the neighbors below them would call the police, so I did feel better for a while. But eventually, the fighting started again. One day, Anna called me and asked me to go down to get Mia. They were fighting again, and this time, David had spit on Anna's face. He had done this before, but I was so mad that day because I had just had enough of both of them. I asked Uncle Ryan to go down with me. My plan was to get you and leave right away. Well, it didn't work out that way. I was getting ready to go get you when David walked up to me from somewhere and started making excuses for his behavior. I was so mad and just tired of it all. I said some really mean things, and then for some reason, I spit right into his face. Ryan jumped out of the car so fast, thinking David would hit me, but David just stood there and looked at me. I think he and Anna were as stunned as I was that I had actually done that. I looked at David, and I asked him, "How does it feel to be spit on?" I must have asked him that three times. Each time with no response, but I wanted him to be as humiliated as my daughter probably felt. Later, I cried for days over it. I felt like the worst person in the world for doing that because that wasn't me. I wasn't someone who ever spit and definitely not on someone. I wrote David a long letter, apologizing for my behavior. I also asked God for forgiveness lots of times, and one day, while praying, God showed me something. David could control his anger. In that one-second act, he could have beaten me to a pulp, but he didn't. He did control his anger with me, so why couldn't he control it with Anna? That was the first time it dawned on me that he was choosing to hit Anna on purpose, and that broke my heart. But I promised myself that I would never lose my control with him or anyone again.

A few weeks later, your parents were fighting, and your dad hit your mom in the face. I just couldn't leave work one more time to deal with this, so I called your grandfather. Your grandfather met up with your dad in the middle of the street in front of Sheetz. Let's just say that your grandfather made it perfectly clear that he would not tolerate your dad touching your mom anymore. I seriously think your grandfather would have ended up in jail if God had not intervened. The day all this happened, I started praying that God would either change David or remove him from our lives.

One day not too long after I started praying for change or removal of your dad, I received a phone call at about 5:00 am one morning, and it was your dad. He told me that he wanted to leave but Anna wouldn't allow him. At this time, you were a year old, and your sister was only five weeks old. This was the game he played. He would pack all his things, and he would go over the mountain to stay with his father and leave your mom alone, crying with you two babies. Then she would get depressed and come stay with us. I ended up tending to you both until she could pull herself together again. Then he would come back, and she would go buy him everything he wanted to prove that she loved him, and the whole cycle would start over again. Through all this, you poor girls were stuck in the middle of the violence. But this particular morning, I decided that I was not getting in the middle. I told your dad to let me talk to your mom. I told Anna that she would let him leave, or I would call the state police. I told her I would also call children's services and have you two girls removed. I told her that I could not and would not do this anymore. I just couldn't. I told her to call me back when David had left. Anna didn't call me back; your dad did. As I talked to him, I told him all the things I told her, then I told him that every day I prayed that God either changed him or remove him. I told him that today was going to be that day because none of us could continue to live this way. I told him that Anna and the girls deserved so much more than what he was doing to them. He did break down on the phone, and he cried. I told him that he had choices to make because today was the day of change. He hung up on me, and I did not talk to him again for two and a half years.

You see, he made a choice. He drove to the city and purchased about two grams of heroin. Then he used some of it, went to a store, and stole a pair of shoes in Williamson. The store called in the theft, and he was arrested. Once he was arrested, they searched his car and found all the drugs. Your dad has been in jail since that day. You see, God answered my prayers based on the choices that David made that day. Some days I feel bad for your dad because he hasn't gotten to see you two grow up, but most days I am thankful to God for where he is because I felt that both of you girls and Anna deserved so much more. The problem with all my feelings back then was that I blamed David for way too much. Both your pappy and I wanted so much for this to be the end of the cycle. It was the end for two and a half years.

ANNETTE RASP

GRACIE

I COULD SPEND hours and hours of writing to tell you about the fights, the drugs, and the drama, but that wouldn't really help you because you wouldn't remember any of it. You were five weeks old when your dad went to jail. The day he went to jail, I truly felt it was the start of a brand-new chapter in your life, your sister's life, and in your mom's. I truly thought that since your dad was getting two to ten years, Anna would move forward, get married to a stable man who could become a strong role model for your girls, and life would be rosy—what a dream for me.

Slowly, Anna did start building a new life. There was a time at the beginning that I didn't think that she would ever get off my couch. She would lie for hours, sleeping with you in her arms. Where I felt that she had never bonded with Mia because of the fighting, you were a whole new story. She seemed to be hanging on to you so tight that sometimes I thought neither of you could breathe.

We knew that Anna was struggling in many ways, but we also knew that we didn't want to give her the easy way out. Your grandfather and I talked at great length about whether we should let her move back home with you girls, but I really felt that would be the wrong thing to do. The hardest thing you ever have to admit is your true feelings, and mine were so hurt from the past that I didn't feel that I could live in the same house with Anna. I loved you girls to death, but I knew that Anna sometimes takes the easy route. The easy route would be to move back in, and I would end up being your only caregiver. At first I thought she would fall apart, but instead she took one day at a time, and she started to improve her life. She changed her job so that she could work daily and make a schedule for you girls. Staying on a schedule did help you all. She also started to take her mental health seriously, and she got on some medicines. It was not always perfect, but every day she was seeing things about herself that was helping her to grow as a good parent.

During these two and a half years, we had some disagreements, mostly about her dragging you two to the prison to see your daddy. But after a while, I realized that she did truly love your daddy, and neither of you seemed upset about the visits. Driving you girls to the prison was a big step for your mom. It took everything she had some days to get you both dressed and loaded for the drive. Up to this point, even driving that far would bring on a panic attack for her. Little by little she started doing things with both of you, little things like going to ball games to see family members, grocery shopping, and just stopping to visit family. All these things she had stopped doing when she and your daddy were living together. All these slowly started to heal some of the hurt between us. So much so that we felt that we could take another big step and help her to buy a house. We wanted so much for her to have a permanent place for you girls to be raised. God truly blessed her with this little house about two miles from us. The payment was no more than she was paying in rent, and it was hers. The whole family helped to paint, clean up, and put new floors down. It really was a place where all of you seemed content.

Once again, it all started to fall apart. Friends from the past always seem to play a part in both Anna's mental and physical relapses. This time, things started to go wrong at the prison where she worked, and the calls started coming again. Anna would call, talking a mile a minute, and I could tell she was having panic attacks. I started to encourage her to go to counseling, but she didn't really want to admit the real issue, which was her fear for her job. Instead, she went back to her old job with all her old friends who had the same old habits, and I started to notice the weight loss (this is always sign #1 that your mother is starting to swing out of control). Next thing we knew, she was fired from the prison for a series of small behavioral issues. Then here comes Max back into her life, the same boy from her senior year that she did drugs with, but now she claimed that he was rehabilitated. Rehabilitation, to me, means being in a program where you are clean and sober, not on a prescription drug that makes you feel the exact same way as the heroin does. They say that heroin is the hardest drug to get off because it causes excruciating physical pain. I have fibromyalgia, so I can understand the pain issue, but I also know that an addict is an addict and that we were in for another painful ride. I do not believe in the whole prescription-drug replacement for an illegal drug. I believe that it can work to get people off drugs if and only if it is monitored strictly, but too many times it is not, and it ends up being just another way to enable people to continue to get high. In my opinion, these drugs end up being a moneymaking deal for drug companies, doctors, and junkies.

Like I said before, your mother always does things out of anger without thinking of the consequences. Somewhere along the line, your daddy, who was in prison, realized before I did that your mom was taking the drug road, so he started writing me letters to talk to her. When I was too thick to get his meaning, he wrote and told me point-blank that Anna was doing heroin. I knew deep in my heart that she was falling back into the drug and alcohol world. I just didn't want to go down this road again, so a part of me just wanted to pretend that it wasn't happening.

I was so hurt, mad, and felt betrayed that I wrote her a letter telling her that I didn't want to be her mother anymore. Everything I said in the letter was the truth, and somewhere in her black-and-white mind, I was hoping that the letter would make her see what she was doing to all of us. The truth is that somewhere over the past two years, I was starting to believe that we could actually become adult friends. I was tired of feeling like I would need to give correction to her life again. In my eyes, she was doing so well, and I was so proud of her and bang-fighting, smashed phones, drugs, and crying babies all over again. Only this time, you, Gracie, have been hurt the most. Mia had already felt the fear and anxiety of the fighting, but you never knew of it, so you started to suffer physically. I've tried to talk to your mom over the months that she has been living with Max, but she doesn't want to hear. I tried to tell her what all this was doing to your emotional health, but the day you crawled up on my lap and said "Nam, I love my mom, but I don't want to go home. Can I stay with you?" broke my heart because the more we talked, the more I realized that you were as afraid of your mom's behavior as you were of her boyfriend. That night, I cried for you like I did when your mom was pregnant with you. When she was pregnant with you, I was so overwhelmed with worry for you because I was scared that you would be born with mental or physical issues because of her random drug use. I would turn on the water, crawl in the tub, and pray and cry for you. I would sometimes sit in there for an hour until I couldn't cry anymore, then I would crawl out and pull myself together because I didn't want your grandfather or Ryan to know how upset I really was. I knew they knew, but sometimes it was just the elephant in the room that no one would talk about. I was so mad at your mother and God. Yet I knew that God's protection was all there was because I couldn't physically do anything to help your mother.

That night, your grandfather and I talked late into the night about everything that was going on, and we decided together that we needed outside help and intervention for you girls. Neither of us could afford to go down this path again or have anything cost us our jobs by ending up with charges for getting involved with their fighting. Once again, we went to talk to children's services, but this time, we did it as a united couple. It has taken a long time for both your grandfather and me to get to complete agreement on issues concerning your mom. But we have reached that point of knowing that we need to be connected for true change to come. If a child can split and divide you as parents, they will. All that does is help them to get their way even if it is harmful to them in the end. The hardest thing we had to do was sit in there and discuss how in four months their fighting has destroyed the home of peace you girls were finally starting to feel. In four months, all the work we had put into changing that house into a home was destroyed by your mom and Max's anger and fighting. Not only emotionally for you two but also physically with broken doors, cracked walls, and broken furniture. All the joy I had when we helped her to purchase the house has now been replaced with sorrow so much so that I can't stand to walk into the house. I prefer not to go there at all.

There has been one blessing through all this mess regarding your daddy. One day, I felt that I needed to drive to the prison to see him. It was probably the hardest thing I ever did because I really didn't know what I was going to say to him after two and half years of silence. I just knew that somewhere in all this, I needed to make peace with him. As I drove there, I prayed a lot about what to say, and I felt in my heart that God just wanted me to tell David who the real me was, not the me that he thought I was and definitely not the me that Anna described me as. I spent three hours with your daddy that day just telling him what was on my heart. I truly felt that we made peace with each other that day as well as peace about the past.

I know that he probably doesn't understand why I continue to write him even after your mother stopped, but somewhere deep in my heart, I felt that he needed a friend. I feel that he needs to know what is happening in your lives. Your mother made a choice to drag you to the prison so that you would know your dad, so I feel that he deserves honesty about your lives. Telling him the truth has not been easy because I have fear that I am stirring up his anger, but writing him has helped me to process the current mess your mom is in. Writing him is sometimes the only hope that I have. Hope that he will see the truth of how all this is affecting you two and hope that he will change and come home and be a better father. I hope that telling him the truth will make him want to come home in protection mode, that he will no longer be the selfish one, and that he will be willing to put his own addictions down for good. A counselor once said that the more stuff that an addict can put between themselves and their addictions, the better off they are to stay clean. I pray that wanting to protect you girls is the stuff that motivates David to stay clean and changed. I know there is always the gamble that it won't work, but I want so much more for you girls, so all I can do is try.

I do believe that time really does heal most wounds if we choose to forgive the past. I'm sure that there are things that will always pop up as blockages. But for me, all I have ever known is this cycle of love and forgiveness with your mother, so I believe that your dad deserves the same process. He is your father, which has made him my family. Included are a few letters that I have written him about your life during this time. Someday I will give you and Mia all of them so that you can see where your dad came from and how much he does love you both. Years ago I might not have said that, but God really does work in mysterious ways. Ever so slowly I am coming to believe that we can make peace even in the midst of storms.

LETTERS TO DAVID

Dear David,

I mailed you a letter today but decided to write another to tell you that I have the girls for the weekend. I really didn't give Anna a choice, and when she didn't respond to me, my mom called her. Anna gets no relief from my family whenever I decide I want them. She told Hope that if she never speaks to me again, it will be too soon. She is really mad because I mailed a paper off the Internet to her and Max about potty training and how wrong it is to discipline children for it. Plus I added a few other comments about the fact that I would contact children's services if I hear any more about it because apparently, they both need to attend some parenting classes. I also told them that disciplining a child for bad behavior really doesn't work; if it did, they wouldn't both be drug addicts now, would they? I told her to choose her battles wisely because I will. The letter, combined with her receiving your letter, pissed Max off so much that he is now refusing to babysit. She apparently had to take the girls to Sam all last week because she wasn't calling me. Anna did tell Hope that Max took off mad and ended up wrecking his motorcycle because of me (of course, they never take responsibility for their own actions). Anna said that she hopes that I never try to talk to her 'cause she has nothing to say to me. Truth is, I don't have much to say to her either, but sometimes she needs to be reminded that I do know what is going on, and she better keep these girls first. I can tell by her cell phone charges that life is not easy for her. Max, apparently, has one old trait of yours: he likes to run off when he is mad. What is it with you boys and running? It really is a bad trait, one I hope that you don't start again when you get out.

You should see Gracie swim. She is like a fish. She can actually swim by herself underwater. Pap about had a heart attack when she took off all by herself. He didn't know she could do that because he wasn't here a couple of weeks ago when she did it. I have to watch her nonstop; she'll jump off the deck and try to swim back to the latter all in one breath. She is something else. Now Mia is a whole different story. She only stays in the water with swimmers on her arms or a ring around her. I can get her to jump, and then I take her under, but she always comes up like she is overwhelmed. They both love the water. I'm sure that is where we will be all day the next couple of days. They need to be outside. The neighbors told me they haven't seen them all week. I'm sure they are outside at Sam's. I hope Sam tries to talk some sense into her.

I know in my heart that Max is going to walk away. Gracie told me that they are still fighting with their fists. When I asked why, Mia said, "'Cause Mom told him to stop smoking in the house and Max hit her." Gracie said, "But Mom hit Max back." It is taking everything in Jacob not to go down there and beat the crap out of him, but I told him to stay away. She is too mad at us, and I don't want to see her have Jacob arrested. It isn't worth it, and I believe that Max would swing at Jacob, and I can tell you this: it would be the worst mistake of his life to swing at Jacob. I'm really glad that Jacob doesn't even know what he looks like. I hope it stays that way.

I continue to pray every day that God heals my family. I just hope it happens sooner than later 'cause it breaks my heart when the girls tell me things like this. There are just some things I can't change. I pray every day about whether to hire a lawyer, and for whatever reason, I feel like I need to wait. I guess that is why I believe so strongly that Max will soon be gone. Anyway, I'll try to take some new pictures and send you soon.

I'm very proud of the progress you are making. Hang in there.

Take care,

Sam

Dear David,

How are you? Good, I hope. Jacob did talk to your dad last week, and he said that he is doing pretty good. Ralph told Jacob that he was waiting on the results of all the tests to see if he would have to do treatments or not. I put money in your account so that you can purchase another phone card if necessary. I didn't know if your dad had set up an account or not. I just felt like you might want to call him or the girls. If you decide to try to call Anna's house, Tuesdays would probably be the best day. That seems to be the day that she is home with the girls alone most times after noon.

We had a little bit of a heated conversation the other day. She always wants to start a conversation, and then she gets mad when I don't say what she wants me to. Well, she got a little bit of an awakening because I told her basically to shut up because I am tired of her tearing me down every time I don't say what she wants to hear. I'm not taking it from her anymore. She always turns on me and tells me that I am telling lies on her, so I asked her, how am I supposed to know the truth when she doesn't even know it? How am I supposed to know it when she changes the story depending on her mood and whom she is talking to? I told her that she has created this mess of a life, and I am not taking responsibility for it anymore. I wasn't the perfect parent and neither was Jacob, but there comes a point in life where you are solely responsible for yourself, and she is well past that point, so she can let the past out of it. If I was such a horrible parent, then be a better one, not a worse one. Needless to say, she left the driveway, screaming at me, but I'm not backing down to her anymore. I told her that if she hates me so much, stay away; it won't hurt my feelings. All I want is to see the girls because I am not raising her anymore, but I love them, and I want to spend time with them. I did the best I could; now her actions are hers, not mine. She can either respect me or stay away. It's her decision. She did send me a text later, apologizing, but her words mean little to me because I'm really tired of Dr. Jekyll/Mr. Hyde mentality. I love my daughter very much, but I can't make her believe it, so I have stopped trying to tell her. Either she knows it by now or she doesn't. She did ask me to help her to get her meds, which I did. Let's hope that means that she will take them and start to see some things in a better light. Anyway, I will continue to pray that God heals my family. I believe in miracles with all my heart, and I truly believe that God is in control. Continue to pray for us.

Well, I better get to work. Use the money as you want. Take care.

Your friend,

Sam

Dear David,

I got your letter today, and I had to laugh because I am struggling with some of the same issues as you are: anger. Let's start with Anna. I am not pushing her to get back with you. I am pushing her to admit the truth. First, she already knew you cheated on her all those years ago when the girls were babies. You might have denied it to her, but in her heart she knew because she told me over and over again when she was crying back then, so I have been pushing her to admit the truth to herself. Second, I have been pushing her to forgive you just as I have asked that of you, but true forgiveness comes from deep within. I have asked God over and over why he wants me to tell you things back here that are seeding your anger in there. Believe me when I say, it's not about the black guys. It's about me and what I am writing; I know that some of the things I write have to be hurting you and making you mad because I am angry. I'm angry because I feel like Anna and Max are you and her four years ago. I'm angry at both God and Anna because Anna has had two and a half years of relative peace where she was doing so good financially as well as emotionally. I'm mad at God more than at Anna because I feel like I did everything he asked me to do in regard to "pushing" both of you to grow up. I did push both of you to walk away because how you were living wasn't healthy for any of you. Then finally, both of you are changing, and she allows anger to destroy it all. Anger over something she already knew.

As for Max, I don't like him because of his actions and words toward the girls. I feel his hatred just standing beside him. He does not care for Anna or the girls. I always knew you loved Anna and she loved you, but him, I don't know what he has to gain by being on this side of the mountain, except for the neighbors saying he is stealing, and if they catch him in the act, they are going to shoot him dead. God gave me a message for Anna to prepare her heart because all that Max was doing in secret was coming to light. I don't know what he is doing, but it's bad, and he is very underhanded. But I will not shed a tear for him or ever write him. The sooner God removes him from their life, the better.

Now you and your struggle, you need to understand that God can only promote us to the next level in his plan for our lives by digging deep into looking at ourselves. These black guys could be Max and your past friends when you get home. Every time you feel anger rising, you need to walk away or silently repeat the action until you make your point across. You are getting stronger every day, but only you can remind yourself of that. Only you can give grace when you want to give a fist; I know I've been there and am still there some days. But I have learned to say to myself constantly, "God, you love me for me, shut my mouth, or give me the right words." I made many mistakes with my relationship with you, and I regret that, but God is giving me this blessing of being your friend now when you need one the most. Sometimes the people fighting against you the most are the ones who will help you to overcome the biggest challenges. I know that when you get out, everything won't be perfect, and we will also see things differently; everyone does. The question is, is everything worth fighting over, or is it worth taking a stand for? Sometimes the biggest success is to follow through with what you believe is right even if you fail—even if you make others mad. Every failure moves you forward or moves you backward. I never want to go backward with you or with Anna; that is why I keep reminding Anna that she is sitting where she is out of anger, not because she cares for Max.

I have started going to a group for parents who have children with drug and alcohol addictions. I am hoping to gain insight into how to help both you and Anna as well as to open up and get some of my own anger out. Pray for me as I will pray for you. Pray for yourself and ask God to help you through this tough time in class.

I'll write you again soon. At the end of the month, I am taking the girls to the circus. That should be fun. I'll have to take some pictures this weekend when I get them. Anna has a wedding to go to, so I am to get them Friday night and Saturday.

Talk to you soon.

Sam

Dear David,

I'm sure you are opening this letter, going, "Who is this picture of, and why is Sam sending this to me?" Well, God put it on my heart to share this story with you and to tell you how much of a blessing your daughters are to her and to me. This picture is my aunt Thelma, my dad's sister, and she is one of my very favorite people. She has been an inspiration to me for most of my life. Mostly because she was diagnosed with cancer twenty-six years ago, and twenty-five years ago, they told her that she only had six months to live. She beat those odds by a lot of years, and she is now eighty years old, but she is going to soon pass away. I've been taking the girls with me every couple of weeks to visit her. She so loves to see them, and every time they go, they ask her what happened to her face, and every time, she tells them. They look at her and say OK. It will be better soon, and she says yes, it will. She knows she is dying this time, but she tells me every time to stop crying because she has been blessed by being born into this family and that I am blessed too, so stop that. I took the girls to her sale Saturday, and later in the evening, Mia thought I was taking a nap, and she got out my anointing oil that I use for prayer, and she was putting it all over her neck and face. As she was doing it, she was saying, "Dear Jesus, please touch Aunt Thelma and make her all better. I love her, so just touch her right now. Amen." I lay there and cried because Mia was so sincere in her heart, and she truly thought no one was listening. To be so innocent in our requests to God is overwhelming to me. Your daughter truly does have a calling in her life. I pray that you and Anna both encourage this in her. But now I want to tell you the other side of Thelma's story because to know this side is to wonder why you would fight cancer for twenty-five years. Thelma's life has not been easy, yet she still calls herself blessed.

Thelma was fourteen years old when she got pregnant with her first child, whom I call Aunt Rose. See, back then, it was not as accepted as it is now, so she had the baby, and my grandmother raised her as her own. I never even knew the truth until twenty years ago. Aunt Rose is actually older than my dad. When Thelma was eighteen, she went off and got married and had three sons. But life wasn't easy because he beat her a lot. After years of that, she filed for divorce, but Pennsylvania law didn't allow you to stay in the same state as the person you were divorcing, so she had to take three young boys and moved to another state. She moved to Maryland and got a nursing job. Eventually, she moved another man in with her, and once again, she picked a man who beat her. By now, the boys were young men. Pete had already enlisted in the military to get away from the fighting, but Luke and Mick were still in high school. Thelma left one relationship but chose not to leave this one for whatever reason, so one day, the boys came home from school and found their mother beaten up pretty bad, so they took a ball bat and beat the man to death. Ann couldn't stop them; they were all bigger than her, so Luke got tried as an adult and was sent to real prison. Mick, being younger, was sent into the youth system until he turned eighteen, then he was automatically being sent into the military. That was the deal they made. Thelma moved back to Pennsylvania in pieces and started driving a tractor and a trailer. This is how she ended up meeting the only uncle I knew, Uncle Bob. By now, she was probably close to fifty; she spent a lot of years trying to help Luke, who was in and out of jail, and Mick, who got out of the service but was now an alcoholic. Uncle Bob was a wonderful man, and he was living whenever the cancer started. She started with one surgery then another, each one taking more and more of her face. But she kept trucking, and one day, Bob and she was sitting at the kitchen table, debating about what time to leave. He said that he had a headache, and she walked into the bathroom to get him something, and when she came back out, he was dead facedown in his breakfast. He had a brain aneurysm that ruptured, so she had to bury the one person whom she truly had peace with. By this time, Luke was out of jail and had actually met a nice lady, and they had three children living with them. But years of being in and out of jail had taken a toll on his health with hepatitis and other things. One day, he told Samantha that he was going rabbit hunting, and he walked out behind the shed and shot himself in the head. So Thelma had to bury a son. Then Mick's life started falling apart, and he was diagnosed with cancer as well as hepatitis from years of heavy drinking. Since he wouldn't take care of himself, his wife divorced him, and within a few years, Aunt Thelma had to bury another son. By now, Thelma has had at least eight facial surgeries for cancer, and now her son Pete has been diagnosed with Agent Orange disease, which will probably take his life too. Yet every time we talk, she tells me that she is blessed. We have talked at great length about her sons and what they did, and she said, "Sam, everyone has a choice in this life. My sons were selfish, and they chose their destiny just like I did mine." She said, "Do not cry for my life, I know God, and he was there every time I needed him to be." She reminds me that I can't change Anna, you, or anyone else, that I can only change me and how I react to each situation. She tells me that I have the right to be mad but not the right to let my anger consume me. She only has two requests: not to die in a hospital, to which I will take a leave off from work to keep her out of one, if needed. The other thing she wants before she dies is to see Luke's children, who are now adults with families in Wyoming. She has not seen them since he killed himself, and Samantha took the kids back to Wyoming because that is where her family was. Thelma is planning to go cross-country with my uncle the last week of this month if the cancer doesn't kill her first.

I tell you all this so that you see that life really is what you make of it. If she sees herself as blessed, shouldn't we? We really are blessed, and we really can change the direction of our lives and our children's. I'm sure that she truly regrets living with abusive men, but I also know that somewhere in this mess of a walk in life, she forgave herself and grew a true relationship with God. One that only she could have. I struggle with minor things most days, and then I visit her and remind myself that my life is minor compared to hers. Just remember that you have your whole life ahead of you. You can influence people for the better. You can change the direction of your life. As she says, change your words and change your life. I hope that her story means something to you. I know it does to me. She will be missed so much by me, but I know that I can enjoy my time with her now, and your daughters love visiting her.

Take care and stay strong.

Sam

Note: My aunt Thelma did make it to Wyoming to see all her grandchildren. Her one grandson, who was stationed in Alaska, was even flown by the military into Wyoming for the visit. I went to visit her two days after her return, and she told me that she was ready to go home to meet her husband. When I got teary eyed, she said, "Stop that and don't cry for me. I have lived a blessed life, and I'm ready to go home." She passed away two weeks later. I will forever remember her as an inspiration to my life.

ANNETTE RASP

Dear David,

How are you? Good, I hope. Well, I no more than sent you the last letter saying that things were quiet, and I went back to work, hoping that things were better. Not so. I received a call from Anna at two o'clock, and she was hysterical, and the girls were screaming and crying in the background. I had to leave and drive down to her house. Needless to say, it was not pretty, and now I feel that all bets are off when it comes to Max. I will not have him around my grandbabies, and if Anna takes him back, I will go to children's services. Matter of fact, I might go anyway because Anna definitely needs bigger help than I can force her into. I already called Max's parole officer, and if he doesn't keep Max on the other side of the mountain, I might just take the girls to the state police.

Here is the story: I got down there, and Anna said that she and Max were fighting about money. He was supposed to give her some for the house payment, which was due Thursday, but he wouldn't hand it over. They got into it, and for some reason, he went and got the girls' blankets. Next thing she knew, he was throwing them in the trash outside. She went in and took them in to wash them because he threw them in a can full of muddy water. He ripped them back from her in the laundry room. In the laundry room, he broke the dresser up and then cut Gracie's blanket to shreds. Anna was trying to get it back, and when he cut it, she lost it and slammed his head into the wall. He got himself up and choked her, slammed her onto the floor, onto the broken dresser. He dragged her across the nails on the broken dresser, and her back was all cut up across her shoulder. Mind you, the girls were watching all this; by the time I got there, he was gone, but before he left, he stole some things, like your watch, a credit card, and some other things that meant something to Anna. Somewhere along the line, she had tried to lock him out, and he had kicked the front door in and broke it. If that wasn't bad enough, she proceeded to tell me how broke she actually was. She has $20 in her checking account and less than $100 in her savings account. Before he moved in, she had about $5,000 saved up for emergencies. Not only did she blow through all that, she took out a second credit card just for him to purchase his prescription medicines on. So she now has two credit cards maxed out. She had almost paid off the Discover one that you and her had run up. Now she is officially $4,000 in credit card debt.

Apparently, his medicines are $106 a week, and she has been paying for them since the day he moved in. So together they blew through $9,000 in five months plus every penny she was earning. Now do you see why he is still there? She is a damn fool. I went through all her bills, and every one is past due. Now the real reason for her pushing him to get a job. She is officially at rock bottom. I went to the bank and put enough money in to pay the house payment that was due. But I won't give her another penny until I know he is gone for good.

Now the part she didn't tell me, the part the girls did. I have had the girls at my house since Wednesday night, and I asked them why Max took their blankets, because Anna never would give me an answer. We had Mia in the kitchen, and we asked her, and she told her pappy and me that when her mommy and Max were fighting, she started crying for me, and Max told her to shut up. When she didn't, Max went into the bedroom and slapped her hard across the face and took both her and Gracie's blankets from them. The rest of the story matched Anna's. Later that night when Gracie, Mia, and I were lying down to go to sleep, I thought Gracie was asleep, so I asked Mia if she was telling me the truth about Max slapping her, and Gracie touched my arm and said, "Nan, Max hit Mia really hard." Up to this point, we had not discussed anything near Gracie or with Gracie because she kept crying about the blanket Max cut up. Thursday morning when I took the kids to Hope's, I drove down Cito Road, and Gracie started crying, saying, "Nan, don't take me home. Max will be there." I told her I wasn't, and she cried the whole way to Hope's. I couldn't get her calmed down. Friday morning when I drove them to Hope's, Max's car was in Anna's driveway as we went past, and both girls started crying, but Mia was having a serious meltdown. I left Hope's and went to the parole officer's office. I told him the whole story, everything, and then we called Max's probation officer together. He recommended that I go from there to children's services, but I didn't because we were leaving to go away for the weekend. I have thought about it all weekend, and if she takes him back, I am turning her in. I will find a way to file a restraining order against him in the girls' name if I have to. They don't want to go home. They haven't seen their mother since Thursday. She has called, and I confronted her about Max being there. She knows I am going to turn her in. She is cleaning the house up, trying to get the smell out of the house. Things are going to be different, and I said yes,

ANNETTE RASP

they are. I didn't tell her anything besides that; she better choose her next steps with Max very carefully.

I'm sorry that I have to tell you all this in writing. I'm sorry that I have to tell you any of this at all, but you need to know the truth. You also need to know that I will do whatever it takes to keep the girls safe even if it means keeping them safe from Anna. I will keep you up-to-date.

Sorry for all the bad news.

Sam

MIA AND GRACIE

OVER THE YEARS, I have asked myself this question many times: What comes first, the chicken or the egg? Mental health issues, domestic abuse, or drugs? Are people born with mental health issues, which make them go to drugs, or do people do drugs because they are so hurt by their childhood that they just want to escape life?

In any case, it doesn't matter to me which comes first. Now it's just about educating both of you on the issues in our lives. Education is important because we need to stop the cycle that keeps going on and on. I wrote all this so that you can understand that we do have to know the past to change the future. Both of you girls will be responsible for your own future. You will be responsible for the choices you make as you get older; even young children have choices to make daily.

I do not know what your future holds in the way of how your parents will be moving forward in life. I can't even promise you that your grandfather and I will handle everything perfectly moving forward, because emotions always play a part in everything we are going through. Sometimes emotions will run too high, and we will probably say and do things we will regret, but I promise you this: your grandfather and I will continue to learn and grow. We will continue to take stands that won't always make us popular if we need to. We all need to learn to do whatever it takes to get us all help. Sometimes the only help that we can get is from outside the family. I don't want you girls to believe that all this behavior is normal. Domestic violence, drug addiction, and mental health issues are serious issues in this world today, so please learn as much as you can to help yourself to not fall into these cycles.

I wrote down a promise that I felt God made me, about healing my family from the inside out. I will continue to pray and believe in that promise. I will try every day to impact your lives (and the lives of your parents) in a positive way. I wrote all this so that someday we can all look back and see how far we have come as individuals as well as a family. I love both of you girls very much. No matter whether you are with me or away from me, know that I am praying for you. Know that I love you for you just as God loves you for you. Know that I want you and your parents to succeed in life. Know that I want you all to be healthy, wealthy, and wise, just as God promised Abraham that his descendants would be. Know that us loving God changes nothing, but knowing how much God loves us changes everything.

Love,

Nam

ADVICE FOR OTHERS

A COUPLE OF THINGS that I would share with others would be the following: If you have children with issues, always discuss them openly and honestly with your spouse even if you are divorced. Be honest with each other and then decide together what plan of action to take regarding your child. So many times we shut out the other person, thinking that they do not understand what is going on, but the truth is that addicts and people with mental health issues manipulate people. Make decisions together then back each other up 100 percent on whatever you agree upon even if it's not the perfect plan. We have come to realize that if we don't stand together, then we go down the path of causing our own marriage/relationships to suffer. We don't always agree totally, but we do make a lot more decisions after honest discussions about how we feel. It has taken us years to both realize how much we truly like as well as love and respect each other. We have decided that we can't allow our family to be split by manipulation anymore.

I recommend counseling or joining church groups for the other children in the family. During the worst of our situation, I took on running the church's youth program. At the time, it didn't seem a smart thing to do, considering all the added stress, but during that time, I realized how much our teenage son, Ryan, was struggling. He was struggling with as much anger and emotions as we were. These emotions were affecting him both at school and at home, and I realized that he also needed counseling. He found a wonderful counselor through the school system, and it helped him tremendously to admit to a stranger that his biggest fear was what-ifs. What if Mom was too late getting there and Mia was dead or Anna was dead? What if Anna followed through with trying to kill herself? Sometimes we get so involved in one child's mess that the other children get left behind. They need an outlet for their emotions just as much as adults do, and sometimes only professionals can help them to talk through their what-if questions. As parents, we want to shelter the younger children and tell them not to talk like that even though we have the same thoughts and don't want to admit to them.

I also recommend support groups for the adults. These groups are very important to help to educate you. If there is one thing I have come to realize, it is that there are many more ways to abuse street drugs, prescription drugs, and alcohol than I ever would have thought imaginable. You can only truly help your children, each other, and yourselves whenever you get educated. Don't take everything for face value; do the research and then seek help.

BORDERLINE PERSONALITY DISORDER

http://en.wikipedia.org/wiki/Borderline_personality_disorder

BORDERLINE PERSONALITY DISORDER (BPD) (according to the ICD-10 World Health Organization disease classification, **emotionally unstable personality disorder, borderline type**) is a personality disorder marked by a prolonged disturbance of personality function, characterized by unusual variability and depth of moods. These moods may secondarily affect cognition and interpersonal relations.

The disorder typically involves an unusual degree of instability in mood and black-and-white thinking, or splitting. BPD often manifests itself in idealization and devaluation episodes and chaotic and unstable interpersonal relationships, issues with self-image, identity, and behavior; as well as a disturbance in the individual's sense of self. In extreme cases, this disturbance in the sense of self can lead to periods of dissociation. It is only recognized by the *Diagnostic and Statistical Manual of Mental Disorders* (DSM-IV) in individuals over the age of 18; however, symptoms necessary to establish the disorder can also be found in adolescents.

Splitting in BPD includes a switch between idealizing and demonizing others (absolute good/love vs. absolute evil/hate with no "grey area"). This, combined with mood disturbances, can undermine relationships with family, friends, and co-workers. BPD disturbances may also include harm to oneself. Without treatment, symptoms may worsen, leading (in extreme cases) to suicide attempts.

There is an ongoing debate among clinicians and patients worldwide about terminology and the use of the word *borderline*, and some have suggested that this disorder should be renamed. The ICD-10 manual has an alternative definition and terminology to this disorder, called *emotionally unstable personality disorder*.

Signs and Symptoms

The primary features of BPD are unstable interpersonal relationships, affective distress, marked impulsivity, and unstable self-image.

Individuals with BPD tend to experience frequent, strong and long-lasting states of aversive tension, often triggered by perceived rejection, being alone or perceived failure. They may show lability (changeability) between anger and anxiety or between depression and anxiety and temperamental sensitivity to emotive stimuli.

The negative emotional states specific to BPD fall into four categories: destructive or self-destructive feelings; extreme feelings in general; feelings of fragmentation or lack of identity; and feelings of victimization.

Behaviour

Individuals with BPD can be very sensitive to the way others treat them, reacting strongly to perceived criticism or hurtfulness. Their feelings about others often shift from positive to negative, generally after a disappointment or perceived threat of abandonment or of losing someone. Self-image can also change rapidly from extremely positive to extremely negative. Impulsive behaviors are common, including alcohol or drug abuse, eating disorders, promiscuous and intense sexuality, gambling and recklessness in general. Attachment studies have revealed a strong association between BPD and insecure attachment style, the most characteristic types being "unresolved," "preoccupied," and "fearful." Evidence suggests that individuals with BPD, while being high in intimacy—or novelty-seeking, can be hyper-alert to signs of rejection or devaluation and tend toward insecure, avoidant or ambivalent, or fearfully preoccupied patterns in relationships. They tend to view the world as generally dangerous and malevolent. BPD is linked to increased levels of chronic stress and conflict in romantic relationships, decreased satisfaction of romantic partners, abuse and unwanted pregnancy; these links may be general to personality disorder and subsyndromal problems.

Manipulation and deceit are viewed as common features of BPD by many of those who treat the disorder as well as by the DSM-IV. Some mental health professionals, however, caution that an overemphasis on these traits and an overly broad definition of "manipulation" can lead to prejudicial treatment of BPD sufferers, particularly within the health care system.

Suicidal or self-harming behavior is one of the core diagnostic criteria in DSM IV-TR, and management of and recovery from this can be complex and challenging. The suicide rate is approximately 8 to 10 percent. Self-injury attempts are highly common among patients and may or may not be carried out with suicidal intent. Ongoing family interactions and associated vulnerabilities can lead to self-destructive behavior. Stressful life events related to sexual abuse can be a particular trigger for suicide attempts by adolescents with BPD tendencies.

DOMESTIC VIOLENCE STATISTICS

- Every 9 seconds in the US a woman is assaulted or beaten.
- Around the world, at least one in every three women has been beaten, coerced into sex or otherwise abused during her lifetime. Most often, the abuser is a member of her own family.
- Domestic violence is the leading cause of injury to women—more than car accidents, muggings, and rapes combined.
- Studies suggest that up to 10 million children witness some form of domestic violence annually.
- Nearly 1 in 5 teenage girls who have been in a relationship said a boyfriend threatened violence or self-harm if presented with a breakup.
- Every day in the US, more than three women are murdered by their husbands or boyfriends.
- Ninety-two percent of women surveyed listed reducing domestic violence and sexual assault as their top concern.
- Domestic violence victims lose nearly 8 million days of paid work per year in the US alone—the equivalent of 32,000 full-time jobs.
- Based on reports from 10 countries, between 55 percent and 95 percent of women who had been physically abused by their partners had never contacted non-governmental organizations, shelters, or the police for help.
- The costs of intimate partner violence in the US alone exceed $5.8 billion per year: $4.1 billion are for direct medical and health care services, while productivity losses account for nearly $1.8 billion.
- Men who as children witnessed their parents' domestic violence were twice as likely to abuse their own wives than sons of nonviolent parents.

Know the Signs

By Mayo Clinic staff

WOMEN AREN'T THE only victims of domestic violence. Understand the signs of domestic violence against men, and know how to get help.

Recognize Domestic Violence against Men

Domestic violence—also known as domestic abuse, battering or intimate partner violence—occurs between people in an intimate relationship. Domestic violence against men can take many forms, including emotional, sexual and physical abuse and threats of abuse. It can happen in heterosexual or same sex relationships.

It might not be easy to recognize domestic violence against men. Early in the relationship, your partner might seem attentive, generous and protective in ways that later turn out to be controlling and frightening. Initially, the abuse might appear as isolated incidents. Your partner might apologize and promise not to abuse you again.

In other relationships, domestic violence against men might include both partners slapping or shoving each other when they get angry—and neither partner seeing himself or herself as being abused or controlled. This type of violence, however, can still devastate a relationship, causing both physical and emotional damage.

You might be experiencing domestic violence if your partner:

- Calls you names, insults you or puts you down
- Prevents you from going to work or school
- Stops you from seeing family members or friends
- Tries to control how you spend money, where you go or what you wear
- Acts jealous or possessive or constantly accuses you of being unfaithful

- Gets angry when drinking alcohol or using drugs
- Threatens you with violence or a weapon
- Hits, kicks, shoves, slaps, chokes or otherwise hurts you, your children or your pets
- Assaults you while you're sleeping, you've been drinking or you're not paying attention to make up for a difference in strength
- Forces you to have sex or engage in sexual acts against your will
- Blames you for his or her violent behavior or tells you that you deserve it
- Portrays the violence as mutual and consensual

Children and Abuse

Domestic violence affects children, even if they're just witnesses. If you have children, remember that exposure to domestic violence puts them at risk of developmental problems, psychiatric disorders, problems at school, aggressive behavior and low self-esteem. You might worry that seeking help could further endanger you and your children, or that it might break up your family. Fathers might fear that abusive partners will try to take their children away from them. However, getting help is the best way to protect your children—and yourself.

Break the Cycle

If you're in an abusive situation, you might recognize this pattern:

- Your abuser threatens violence.
- Your abuser strikes you.
- Your abuser apologizes, promises to change and offers gifts.
- The cycle repeats itself.

Typically the violence becomes more frequent and severe over time.

Domestic violence can leave you depressed and anxious. You might be more likely to abuse alcohol or drugs or engage in unprotected sex. Domestic violence can even trigger suicide attempts. Because men are traditionally thought to be physically stronger than women, you might be less likely to talk about or report incidents of domestic violence in your heterosexual relationship due to embarrassment or fear of ridicule. You might also worry that the significance of the abuse will be minimized because you're a man.

Similarly, a man being abused by another man might be reluctant to talk about the problem because of how it reflects on his masculinity or because it exposes his sexual orientation. Additionally, if you seek help, you might confront a shortage of resources for male victims of domestic violence. Health care providers and other contacts might not think to ask if your injuries were caused by domestic violence, making it harder to open up about abuse. You might also fear that if you talk to someone about the abuse, you'll be accused of wrongdoing yourself. Remember, though, if you're being abused, you aren't to blame—and help is available.

Start by telling someone about the abuse, whether it's a friend, relative, health care provider or other close contact. At first, you might find it hard to talk about the abuse. However, you'll also likely feel relief and receive much-needed support.

IS IT DEPRESSION OR JUST THE BLUES?

http://www.webmd.com/depression/is-it-depression-or-the-blues

S OONER OR LATER, everyone gets the blues. Feeling sadness, loneliness, or grief when you go through a difficult life experience is part of being human. And most of the time, you can continue to function. You know that in time you will bounce back, and you do.

But what if you don't bounce back? What if your feelings of sadness linger, are excessive, or interfere with your work, sleep, or recreation? What if you're feeling fatigue or worthlessness, or experiencing weight changes along with your sadness? You may be experiencing major depression.

Also known as clinical depression, major depressive disorder, or unipolar depression, major depression is a medical condition that goes beyond life's ordinary ups and downs. Almost 18.8 million American adults experience depression each year, and women are nearly twice as likely as men to develop major depression. People with depression cannot simply "pull themselves together" and get better. Treatment with counseling, medication, or both is key to recovery.

Major Depression: What Are the Symptoms?

Depression shows itself in different ways. Common depression symptoms are:

- Depressed mood, sadness, or an "empty" feeling, or appearing sad or tearful to others
- Loss of interest or pleasure in activities you once enjoyed
- Significant weight loss when not dieting, or significant weight gain (for example, more than 5% of body weight in a month)
- Inability to sleep or excessive sleeping
- Restlessness or irritation (irritable mood may be a symptom in children or adolescents too), or feelings of "dragging"
- Fatigue or loss of energy
- Feelings of worthlessness, or excessive or inappropriate guilt

- Difficulty thinking or concentrating, or indecisiveness
- Recurrent thoughts of death or suicide without a specific plan, or a suicide attempt or specific plan for committing suicide

Depression Treatment: When Should You Get Help?

If you have five or more of these symptoms for most of the day, nearly every day, for at least two weeks, and the symptoms are severe enough to interfere with your daily activities, you may have major depression. It's important to talk to your doctor about treatments to start helping you feel better.

ATTENTION DEFICIT HYPERACTIVITY DISORDER

http://www.webmd.com/add-adhd/guide/adhd-symptoms

THE SYMPTOMS OF ADHD include inattention and/or hyperactivity and impulsivity. These are traits that most children display at some point or another. But to establish a diagnosis of ADHD, sometimes referred to as ADD, the symptoms should be inappropriate for the child's age.

ADHD is common in children and teens. Adults also can have ADHD. With ADHD in adults, there may be some variation in symptoms. For instance, an adult may experience restlessness instead of hyperactivity. In addition, adults with ADHD consistently have problems with interpersonal relationships and employment.

Types of ADHD

There are three different types of ADHD, including:

- combined ADHD (the most common type), which involves all of the symptoms
- inattentive ADHD (previously known as ADD), which is marked by impaired attention and concentration
- hyperactive-impulsive ADHD, which is marked by hyperactivity without inattentiveness

For a diagnosis of ADHD, some symptoms that cause impairment must be present before age seven. Also, some impairment from the symptoms must be present in more than one setting. For instance, the person may be impaired at home and school or home and work. Also, there must be clear evidence the symptoms interfere with the person's ability to function at home, in social environments, or in work environments.

Symptoms of ADHD

There are three different categories of ADHD symptoms: inattention, hyperactivity, impulsivity.

Inattention may not become apparent until a child enters the challenging environment of school. In adults, symptoms of inattention may manifest in work or in social situations.

A person with ADHD may have some or all of the following symptoms:

- difficulty paying attention to details and tendency to make careless mistakes in school or other activities; producing work that is often messy and careless
- easily distracted by irrelevant stimuli and frequently interrupting ongoing tasks to attend to trivial noises or events that are usually ignored by others
- inability to sustain attention on tasks or activities
- difficulty finishing schoolwork or paperwork or performing tasks that require concentration
- frequent shifts from one uncompleted activity to another
- procrastination
- disorganized work habits
- forgetfulness in daily activities (for example, missing appointments, forgetting to bring lunch)
- failure to complete tasks such as homework or chores
- frequent shifts in conversation, not listening to others, not keeping one's mind on conversations, and not following details or rules of activities in social situations

Hyperactivity symptoms may be apparent in very young preschoolers and are nearly always present before the age of seven. Symptoms include:

- fidgeting, squirming when seated
- getting up frequently to walk or run around
- running or climbing excessively when it's inappropriate (in teens this may appear as restlessness)
- having difficulty playing quietly or engaging in quiet leisure activities
- being always on the go
- often talking excessively

ANNETTE RASP

Hyperactivity may vary with age and developmental stage.

Symptoms of ADHD continued . . .

Toddlers and preschoolers with ADHD tend to be constantly in motion, jumping on furniture, and having difficulty participating in sedentary group activities. For instance, they may have trouble listening to a story.

School-age children display similar behavior but with less frequency. They are unable to remain seated, squirm a lot, fidget, or talk excessively.

In adolescents and adults, hyperactivity may manifest itself as feelings of restlessness and difficulty engaging in quiet sedentary activities.

Impulsivity symptoms include:

- impatience
- difficulty delaying responses
- blurting out answers before questions have been completed
- difficulty awaiting one's turn
- frequently interrupting or intruding on others to the point of causing problems in social or work settings
- initiating conversations at inappropriate times

Impulsivity may lead to accidents such as knocking over objects or banging into people. Children with ADHD may also engage in potentially dangerous activities without considering the consequences. For instance, they may climb to precarious positions.

Many of these symptoms occur from time to time in normal youngsters. However, in children with ADHD they occur frequently—at home and at school or when visiting with friends. They also interfere with the child's ability to function normally.

ADHD is diagnosed after children consistently display some or all of the above behaviors in at least two settings, such as at home and in school, for at least six months.

Long-Term Prognosis with ADHD

Some children with ADHD—approximately 20% to 30%—develop learning problems that may not improve with ADHD treatment. Hyperactive behavior can be associated with the development of other disruptive disorders, particularly conduct and oppositional-defiant disorder. Why this association exists is not known.

A great many children with ADHD ultimately adjust. Some, though, especially those with an associated conduct or oppositional-defiant disorder, are more likely to drop out of school. These individuals fare more poorly in their later careers than individuals who did not have ADHD do.

Inattention tends to persist through childhood and adolescence and on into adulthood. The symptoms of hyperactivity and impulsivity tend to diminish with age.

As they grow older, some teens that have had severe ADHD since middle childhood experience periods of anxiety or depression.

There are several warning signs for ADHD that seem to get worse when demands at school or home increase. They include:

- difficulties following instructions
- being unable to get organized, either at home or at school
- fidgeting, especially with the hands and feet
- talking too much
- failing to finish projects, including chores and homework
- not paying attention to and responding to details
- getting poor grades in school
- being isolated from peers due to poor grades and secondary depression

DRUG ADDICTION FACTS

http://www.michaelshouse.com/drug-addiction/the-statistics/and Statistics

THE INFORMATION BELOW pertains to drug addiction and drug abuse in the United States—both a national and state-by-state level.

- In 2010 there was an estimated 22.6 million Americans over the age of 12 that were current or former illicit drug users within the last month of when the survey was given; This equates to about 8.9 percent of the population aged 12 or older.
- The drug marijuana was the most commonly used illegal substance. There was about 17.4 million individuals who used it in the past month from when the survey was taken. From 2007 and 2010, those numbers increased to 6.9 percent, up from 5.8 or 14.4 million to 17.4 million users.
- Individuals 50 to 59 years of age, their rate of past drug use went up from 2.7 percent to 5.8 percent from 2002 to 2010
- An estimated 10.0 million individual 12 to 20 years of age that admitted to being drinkers; 6.5 million were binge drinkers and 2.0 million heavy drinkers.
- Over six million children in America live with at least one parent who has a drug addiction.
- Since 1980, the number of deaths related to drug overdoses has risen over 540 percent.
- The most commonly abused drug (other than alcohol) in the United States by individuals over the age of 12 is Marijuana, followed by prescription painkillers, cocaine and hallucinogens.
- Each year, drug abuse and drug addiction cost employers over 122 billion dollar in lost productivity time and another 15 billion dollars in health insurance costs.
- Baltimore, Maryland has more per capita individuals living with heroin addiction than any other state in the U.S.
- Since 1990, the number of individuals who take prescription drugs illegally is believed to have risen by over 500 percent.

WHAT ARE THE MOST COMMON DRUG ADDICTION SYMPTOMS?

EVERY DRUG IS different, and so too are the symptoms associated with various addictions. The following signs and symptoms tend to run across most major drug addictions.

- **Mood swings.** Drug addiction can elicit a wide range of emotions in the individual. They may experience feelings of euphoria and excitement when under the influence, but then "crash" to the lowest of depressive states when in between doses. These mood swings can have a significant impact on the individual and those closest to them.
- **Nervousness.** Many drug addicts are constantly nervous or seem restless. In between doses of their drug they may find it difficult to sit still. Or in the case of cocaine addiction or other stimulant dependence, the effects of the drug itself may cause nervous behavior.
- **Illness.** Drug abuse is not a healthy lifestyle. Many people will see several different aspects of their physical health suffer as a result. In addition to the strain that drug addiction puts on the liver, heart, kidneys and other vital internal organs, overdose is a constant threat and one that can land the individual in the hospital for an extended period of time.
- **Sleeplessness.** Individuals with a drug addiction are often unable to sleep through the night. They may suffer from insomnia or will be incredibly difficult to wake up in the morning.
- **New peer groups.** Many addicts will forgo their old friends and valued relationships in exchange for a new peer group that is more accepting of drug use.
- **Criminal activity.** Many drug-addicted individuals find themselves in trouble with the law. In addition to the illegal nature of the substances themselves, many will engage in criminal behavior while

under their influence (including driving while intoxicated, robbery or theft to support one's habit, drug dealing, etc.) or in search of their next "fix."

- **Premature death.** While not technically a symptom of drug addiction, it is all too often the end-result. Many drug addicts see their health deteriorate quickly, or fall victim to a drug overdose.

www.ingramcontent.com/pod-product-compliance
Lightning Source LLC
Chambersburg PA
CBHW020346290526
45785CB00005B/2170